Essence o...

# Essence of Prayer

Ruth Burrows

burns & oates

Burns & Oates

The Tower Building
11 York Road
London SE1 7NX

80 Maiden Lane
Suite 704
New York
NY 10038

*www.continuumbooks.com*

*Grateful thanks to Sister Gillian ocd who collected and prepared
these essays for the publisher.*

First published 2006

Reprinted 2006, 2007

British Library Cataloguing-in-Publication Data
A catalogue record for this book is available from the
British Library.

ISBN 0 8601 2425 8

Typeset by Free Range Book Design & Production Ltd.

Printed and bound in Great Britain by MPG Ltd, Bodmin,
Cornwall

# Contents

# Foreword

It has been said that each age gets the authors it deserves. This is obviously not true. How did the Elizabethans come to deserve Shakespeare, whereas we receive X and Y (names withheld out of compassion)? What doomed Victorians to those heavy tomes of pious exhortation, so religiously read, whereas we, in our noisy, destructive, foolish century, are blessed with Ruth Burrows and her life-enhancing clarities?

'Blessing' is the only appropriate description of such a book as the one you are now holding. One could argue that every spiritual book is a blessing: even if we gain nothing helpful from it, the mere desire to come closer to God, our search for Him, means, as always, that 'those who seek, find'.

But to read Ruth Burrows is not to be technically blest. It is to take into your mind and heart the insight of somebody who is close to God, and has the rare ability to share that closeness with others. God has given her great gifts, and she has opened herself to receive them. He has given her intellectual brilliance so that her mind moves with ease and certainty between concepts. He has given her literary grace, so that what she writes is delightful to read, witty in its expression, persuasive in its idiom, poetic at times, always forceful.

These gifts she was born with. But her greatest gift, again purely from God, is to have received His love. Ruth Burrows has understood, at an exceptional depth, that 'God' for us can only mean Jesus: 'no one can come to the Father except through me'. She has accepted to live by what Jesus is, with all it implies. For her personally, it has meant suffering. Her faith is sustained by the Lord alone: she has no feedback. Emotional reassurances are a consolation indeed, but they are not of the essence, and the truth of this she has lived over many stark years in Carmel.

We support our faith by reading, by discussion, through the sacraments, by earnestly trying to live it: it is the basis, and the only basis, of our prayer. But the life we live of devotion and practice depends only on Jesus and not on self. Every line Ruth Burrows writes is a testament to this.

As we read, the immense practicality of her commitment becomes ever more compelling. Does it not inspire us to follow her example? But 'her example' is not so much in herself, as in being a conduit to allow the Spirit of Jesus to flow through her, and in that she gives us the truest example of all.

SISTER WENDY BECKETT
Quidenham
October 2005

# CHAPTER ONE

# Some Reflections on Prayer

*Starting off on the right foot*

Prayer. We take the word for granted but ought we to do so? What do we mean by prayer? What does the word mean in the Christian context? Almost always when we talk about prayer we are thinking of something *we* do and, from that standpoint, questions, problems, confusion, discouragement, illusions multiply. For me, it is of fundamental importance to correct this view. Our Christian knowledge assures us that prayer is essentially what *God* does, how God addresses us, looks at us. It is not primarily something we are doing to God, something we are giving to God but what God is doing for us. And what God is doing for us is giving us the divine Self in love.

*God – total Love, total Gift*

Any talk about prayer, if we are to stand in the clear, pure atmosphere of truth, must begin by reflecting in firm belief on what Jesus shows us of God. Let us push straight to the heart of the matter. What is the core, the central message of the revelation of Jesus? Surely it is of the unconditional love of God for us, for each one of us: God, the unutterable, incomprehensible Mystery, the Reality of all reality, the Life of all life. And this means that divine Love desires to communicate Its Holy Self to us. Nothing less! This is God's irrevocable will and purpose; it is the reason why everything that is, is, and why each of us exists. We are here to receive this ineffable, all-transforming, all beatifying Love. Well-instructed Christians know this notionally but, alas, few know it really. And here I must add an important reminder that knowing it 'really' does not imply 'feelingly'. To know really – or really to know – means living that knowledge, living out of it. It means that our way of looking at things, our attitudes, our actions arise from this knowledge. Of this real knowledge we use the word faith. This must give us pause and make us very cautious of claims to faith. 'Of course I have faith!' We can feel quite indignant if someone implies otherwise! My experience tells me that real faith is rare and it is best we acknowledge this so that we may really work at believing.

*God – or ego?*

Basing ourselves, therefore, on what Jesus shows us of God (and we Christians have only one teacher,

Jesus the Christ, who is our Way), we must realize that what we have to do is allow ourselves to be loved, to be there for Love to love us. It cannot be a matter of our finding some way of contacting God, of making God real to us, of getting hold of a secret key with which to open the mystic door. Nor is this faith in Jesus our Way compatible with such distressed meanings as: 'I can't pray' or 'my prayer is hopeless' or 'I have never had anyone to teach me how to pray and therefore I don't pray.' When we find ourselves dissatisfied or anxious about our prayer it is worth asking ourselves the question: 'What do I *really* want?' and trying to listen honestly to the answer. We can be fairly certain that it will be some kind of ego-satisfaction. I may want to feel I am making progress, that my prayer is 'working' or that I am a spiritual adept. I may want to feel I am getting something for my money! True prayer means wanting GOD not ego. The great thing is to lay down this ego-drive. This is the 'life' we must lose, this the 'self' we must abandon if we are to have true life and become that self God wants us to be, which only God can know and ultimately only God can bring into being. We have to recognize that a great deal that goes for interest in and longing for prayer is a subtle form of self-seeking. To give ourselves seriously to prayer is to recognize this and face up to the choice it presents: will we cast aside our egotism, allow God's love to purify it more and more whatever the cost, or will we camouflage it, give it other, more spiritual names, and look around for so-called spiritual guides who will offer us ego-satisfying techniques with the promise of an 'experience'. Perhaps we give up the prayer-project altogether with the reflection that, after all, what matters is living and loving and serving our neighbour. Another very popular form of evasion is just to go on worrying and asking endless questions about prayer with the illusory aim that one fine day we will be shown 'how to do it.' The thing to do is, of course, to get down to praying! That will answer our questions.

### Get out of the boat; walk on the waters with Jesus

Let us assume that we do want God or, at least, we want to want God, wobbly and weak though we know ourselves to be. 'If it is you, bid me come to you upon the waters.' (Mt. 14.28) It *is* the Lord and he says: 'Come!' So we can confidently enter into the Mystery that is God, relying solely on Jesus and not at all on ourselves. To enter into real prayer, prayer that opens us to the mystical dimension is, in one sense, to enter into an alien element. At least, it is experienced as such, though, if we are faithful we shall discover that it is in fact our true home. But we have to be willing to let go of our own criterion of what prayer is and what growth in the Spirit might mean. There are all sorts of ways of praying and there are books galore to direct us on them; yet these, at bottom, keep us in the boat. The boat might rock a bit and feel uncomfortable at times; but at least, with our method to guide us, we can man it and have some

4

control. Real prayer lets go of the controls, or, more truly, lets go when they are wrenched away from us, and how often we experience this, even to being tipped out in a squall. Oh dear! Most of us see this as an unfortunate occurrence that must never be repeated and so we refit our boat, and improve our sailing skills to ensure that we have control once more.

## Methods are not Prayer

What does it mean in practice to say we must be there for God and let God control our prayer, let God act? Does it mean we remain inert, completely passive? No, decidedly not! The essential thing we have to do is *believe* in the enfolding, nurturing, transforming Love of God which is *the* Reality: the Reality that is absolutely, totally there whether we avert to It or not. Prayer, from our side, is a deliberate decision to avert to It, to respond to It in the fullest way we can. To do this we must set time aside to devote exclusively to the 'Yes' of faith.

> God of Thy goodness, give me Thyself: for Thou art enough to me, and I may nothing ask that is less that may be full worship to Thee; and if I ask anything that is less, ever me wanteth – but only in Thee I have all.
>
> (Julian of Norwich, *Revelations of Divine Love*, ch.5)

If we are convinced that this is the heart of prayer, this basic decision to remain open to the inflowing

5

of divine love, then we shall understand that we can choose any method we like to help us maintain this basic desire and intention. Our troubles and distress arise from our instinctive assumption that the method is the prayer, and so we gauge the genuineness and success of the prayer by how well the method has worked.

## God's Secret

We must remember that prayer takes place at the deepest level of our person and escapes our direct cognition; therefore we can make no judgement about it. It is God's holy domain and we may not usurp it. We have to trust it utterly to God. This is one of the principle ways in which we surrender control and 'walk on the water'. We must be ready to believe that 'nothingness' *is* the presence of divine Reality; emptiness is a holy void that Divine Love is filling. Remember, we are casting ourselves wholly on Jesus, on his 'Come!' We must give up wanting assurances either from within or without. You see, we cannot have it both ways!

## Prayer versus Achievement

To maintain this simple, trusting exposure to divine Love inevitably means resisting the temptation to 'make a success' of prayer. We could, for instance (depending on our temperament), repeat a mantra with such concentration that our thoughts did not wander, or we might, perhaps, enter into a mesmerized, suspended state, or even achieve some sort of 'experience'. But an experience of what? We could give ourselves up to fascinating reflections on a passage from the Bible, our thoughts so gripped, so uplifted that they did not wander. This is not prayer. Here we touch on what is, in practice, a tricky issue. To repeat a mantra (i.e. a short prayer) can be an excellent way of helping us to focus on receiving God's love. So, too, can reflection on a Scripture text. Most of us certainly need some support to keep us there. But we must learn to distinguish between making use of a support and of substituting the support for prayer. Keeping our deepest heart exposed, refusing to usurp God's place by making ourselves the agent, the giver, will mean that, most often, we have no sense of having prayed well or having prayed at all. I am convinced that, if we are sincere in our desire for God and are willing to pay the price, we can listen to our heart of hearts and know that it's all right and go on quietly in trust. Many times it has been said to me by those who have come to understand real prayer: 'How different it is from what I thought and what people in general think it is!' Jesus, God's revelation, has turned our merely human, worldly expectations upside down. Learning true prayer means learning to die in the sense Jesus meant by this: dying to egotism, self-determination and self-achieving, and letting God recreate us in love in a way that only God can do.

## Union

Committing ourselves to this faith-filled, exposed and selfless prayer ensures that divine Love can work in us the blessed work of union. A profound, obscure knowledge of God will be infused into us and with it a passion of love. This has nothing, of itself, to do with feeling but it means that God does indeed become the passion of our life; that we do, most truly, live for God and fulfil our divine vocation to be for the praise of his glorious love. (cf. Eph. 1.6) The inflowing of God into our secret depths of its very nature must remain secret, as John of the Cross tirelessly insists: '... it happens secretly in darkness, hidden from the faculties ... so hidden that the soul cannot speak of it.' But its effect on our life will be marked and perhaps the umbrella word here could be *selflessness*. The fruits of the Holy Spirit abound in the selfless heart.

## Nourishing faith on the Word

If we are to persevere in constant believing, we need nourishment. The Word is the normal source of nourishment and the Word above all others is the Jesus-Word: what he did, how he was, what he said. Here – and in the letters of Paul and others – is where we learn what God, the ineffable Beauty and Love to whom we are surrendering ourselves, is truly like. Scripture is not easily understood; we have to approach it with faith and we have to work for it to yield its meaning. There are, of course, excellent books of consummate scholarship to help us in our understanding if we have the time, capacity and opportunity to avail ourselves of them. But a rich source of theology and prayer at hand for each of us is the Missal. Here we find theology at its purest, theology that is prayed, that *is* prayer. If we were to absorb the contents of the Missal we would need little else. Study the four Eucharistic Prayers, the Prefaces throughout the yearly seasons and the great doxology 'Glory to God in the Highest.' Look carefully at the Collects, especially the one so easily overlooked, the 'Prayer over the Offerings.' Then, of course, there are the daily readings from the Old and New Testaments with verses from the psalms: a wealth of prayed theology, the Church's understanding at its purest consisting of treasures old and new.

## The Mass: the prayer that is Jesus

Another great advantage of this study of the Missal is that it will deepen our understanding of the Mass, the central act of our worship. This is the supreme prayer, since it is the sacrament of Jesus' perfect prayer, that of his very being as he surrendered in passionate love to his Father in his death on the cross. Expressed in this sacrament is all that we mean by mystical prayer. It is our precious Catholic inheritance to realize that the essence of worship and prayer must always lie with God's Self-communication to us and that our part is merely response. We who know Jesus do not depend on our own prayers, our own ways of getting in touch with God, pleasing him, atoning for our sins and so forth. We know that all this has been given for us in Jesus. We have to go and claim it. The fountain is there for us, overflowing, and all that we have to do is drink. We notice in the Mass prayers how we are, so to speak, continually 'mingling' with Jesus, immersing ourselves in what he is doing. Our offering of ourselves is to become one with the perfect offering of Jesus. We too are to become the perfect offering that the Father lovingly accepts, an offering that is first and foremost God's own gift to us. O marvellous exchange!

CHAPTER TWO

# Growth in Prayer

As soon as we talk or write about prayer and
growth in prayer we are faced with huge difficulties. We are talking and writing, not merely
about the deepest thing in human life, but about its
very essence, about the mystery of God himself. We
are daring to use terms such as 'intimacy' and
'friendship' since it is beyond doubt, for the
believer, that this is to what we are called. We find
a breathing of it in the first pages of Genesis where,
it is intimated, God was wont to walk with his man
and woman through the garden in the cool of the
day. Though sin came to rupture this blessed state,
still, throughout the pages of the Old Testament
with its history of human beings as they really are
– sinful, blind, obstinate, hard of heart – there
shine stars, 'friends of God,' who in some measure
attained, or were granted, intimacy with the awe-
ful mystery. Such intimacy is still possible. Even
amidst a perverse and corrupt people: 'Enoch
walked with God; and he was not, for God took
him.' (Gen. 5.24) Here, it is suggested, was
someone for whom God meant so much that he

11

was swallowed up by him. Enoch disappeared; only God shone out. In this pregnant phrase of scripture we have a summing up of holiness, of the perfection of a human life.

Moses spoke with God face to face, and through this terrible exposure was transformed in such a way that he became 'God' for the people at large, a people too sensual and selfish to want God himself. They were not prepared to pay the price.

> ... we have heard his voice out of the midst of the fire; we have this day seen God speak with man and man still alive. Now therefore, why should we die? For this great fire will consume us; if we hear the voice of the Lord our God any more, we shall die. For who is there of all flesh, that has heard the voice of the living God speaking out of the midst of fire, as we have, and has still lived? Go near, and hear all that the Lord God will say; and speak to us all that the Lord our God will speak to you; and we will hear it and do it. (Deut. 5.24–27)

This is an authentic human cry. If we use the term 'friendship with God' then we must know what we are doing, we must speak with utmost seriousness and with deep awe. There is no place for flippancy or trifling. What did it mean for Enoch? What did it mean for Moses? And, we shall ask, what did it mean for Jesus – to be a friend of God, to be on that lonely, dreadful mountain exposed to we know not what? And yet intimacy with God is the blissful fulfilment of us all. It is what we were made for and for what we endlessly yearn. It is to this that we blindly reach out in our human search for

12

friendship and intimacy. But whereas even the richest human friendship, even that which has truly made one flesh of two, is only part of an existence and life, our relationship with God is our very meaning as human beings. The human creature is, by definition, a relation to God. We become human, become what we are meant to be, in the measure that, like Enoch of old, we are lost to ourselves and taken up into him. Prayer, on our side, is a conscious affirmation of this truth: an effective desire and willing that it be accomplished.

How do we attain to intimacy with God? Or, rather, how do we enter into the intimacy offered? We must be certain that no wooing is necessary. We do not have to find ways of attracting the divine partner, of getting him to notice us. Here is someone who is love itself, the very fount of our existence, enfolding us, inviting us to receive him, drawing us to his heart. All these human expressions are totally inadequate. Scripture and mystical writers have used the different modes of human love and friendship – parent/child, husband/wife, brother/friend – to tell us something of the reality of God's love and desire for us. Each is inadequate. All together they are inadequate. It is not easy to speak properly of a deep human relationship: how much more so when one of the partners is God. And even if one were able, through profound experience and intense thought and effort, to give what seems to be as close an approximation to the truth as possible, its understanding depends on the heart of the recipient. Truth must find an echo in the one who hears if it is to be recognized.

Put it another way: a heart must be really listening, really wanting the truth, really wanting God. The difficulty is that we do not want him. We want our own version of him, one we can, so to speak, carry around in our pockets rather as some superstitious people carry around a charm. We can hold endless, loving conversations with this one, feel we have an intimate understanding with him, we can tell him our troubles, ask for his approbation and admiration, consult him about all our affairs and decisions and get the answer we want, and this God of ours has almost nothing to do with God!

Most of us find it almost impossible not to think of prayer as a special activity in life: an art that can be taught or learned rather as we can learn to play a musical instrument. Because of this, some of us are quick to feel we are proficient, others that we are painfully handicapped, are missing out on some secret or have some lack in our nature which makes prayer difficult if not impossible for us. We feel there are certain laws governing prayer, and techniques to be mastered, and, when we have got hold of these, we can pray. Thus we tend to look around for the guru, for the one who has mastered the art and its techniques, and eagerly look to be taught. When we take up a book or article on prayer, we shall probably detect, if we stop to think, that we are looking for the key, the magic formula that is going to put our prayer right, enable us 'to make a go' of this mysterious activity called prayer. We may feel that others seem to take it in their stride but somehow it does not work for us, and anxiously we look hither and thither for someone who will hand us the secret. All this is proof enough that we are overlooking the fundamental fact: that prayer is not a technique but a relationship. There is no handicap, no obstacle, no problem. The only problem is that we do not want God. We may want a 'spiritual life', we may want 'prayer', but we do not want God. All anyone can do for us, any guru can teach us, is to keep our eyes on Jesus, God's perfect, absolute friend.

If we look at the Gospels we shall find that Jesus never speaks of us as being friends of God. He teaches us to call him Father. Friend implies equality of status; 'child' or 'son' implies total dependence and absolute obedience. When Jesus gave us his own privilege of calling God '*Abba*' that word certainly carried with it everything we understand of the unbreakable, utterly reliable, tender, compassionate, infinitely involved fatherly/ motherly love of God. Of this we must be sure to the marrow of our bones. But equally we must remember what the father-son relationship was in the Jewish culture of Jesus' time. We can go so far as to say that the son was considered as having no life or even existence of his own. He owed absolutely everything to the father. We might even say that a son was his father's 'thing' owing him total, unconditional obedience. When Jesus tells us that we must call God *Abba,* and live as his children, he is demanding of us this decentralization and 'ek-stasy', this standing-out-of-self, in order to transfer our existence, our meaning, our importance, our weight, to the Father. It is a summons to the most radical self-denial.

15

On the other hand, Jesus gives us the title 'friend', his friend, in that we have opened ourselves to and received his revelation of the Father, trusting him with our lives, obeying him as Jesus did. To become the friend of Jesus means to identify with his own life for his Father. This alone is prayer; this alone is intimacy with God. Its blissful fulfilment remains as hidden from our sight and experience as it was for Jesus in his earthly life. All that concerns us here and now is what concerned Jesus: that God should have just whatever he wants. Jesus has become our Way, our Truth and our Life because he declined to have any way of his own, any truth or reality of his own, only the Father's. He declined to live from his own wellspring but only from the Father. This is what we have to do; this is how we must live.

Jesus is with us always, not so as to pillow our weary heads on his breast and continually murmur words of solace in our ears, but so as to share with us his vision, his passionate dedication to the Father's will. He is with us to brace, reinforce, underpin us for our life's great task. True, he lifts from our shoulders the crushing yoke of an alien master, the god we have fashioned in our own likeness, by revealing to us the true face of the Father. He breaks off self-made shackles of bondage and sets us free. Thus his companionship gives us rest and real happiness. Nevertheless there remains a yoke and a burden that has to be carried with courage and love. Life-giving, joy-giving knowledge of Jesus and of the Father he reveals does not drop into our lap from heaven. We have to work for it. 'Come to me', says Jesus, and we must go to him. And the prime way of going to him is by intent, loving absorption of Scripture, particularly the New Testament. Put simply: we must strive to acquire an intellectual knowledge of him, of his attitudes, values and teaching. This intellectual knowledge is certainly not intimacy, certainly not a 'knowing Jesus', but it is an indispensable ingredient for intimacy and real knowing. It is work we have to do, a practical expression of our earnest desire to get to know our Lord. Moreover, it supplies, so to speak, the matter into which spirit can be infused. Or, in more homely words: we laboriously gather the faggots to build the bonfire that only God can set alight. But it has to be there for him to set alight. And we must realize that it is not a case of our having to labour all by ourselves until the bonfire is a good size and everything well-dried out, and then we can hope for God to set fire to it. No, we are never working alone. When we search for him in the Scriptures we have already found him. He is with us, at a level we do not perceive and cannot perceive, touching our inmost depth and working within us, infusing light, inflaming the will. From time to time we may be aware of enlightenment and a stirring of desire, but it is utter folly to conclude that, if we do not feel those things 'it has not come off' or, 'I am getting nowhere.' That might be so were we engaged in secular study, or even in sacred Scripture in a secular way, but it is certainly not so when we are listening to the Word of God, whether it be in our private reflection or in the communal form of listening in the liturgy. We are engaged in a sacramental action. Something is happening just as it happens in the Eucharist and other sacraments. But, as with them, our part is essential. We must bring our elements to it. 'Seek and you *will* find,' Jesus assures us solemnly. Our seeking in Scripture must be like that of the bride in the Song of Songs: all heart, never a merely intellectual effort. Our heart must infuse our minds with trust, desire, resolution. Our heart must be in our eyes as we read and in our ears as we hear. Most certainly we shall find him.

This search for the beloved in the revealed Word means that our times of silent prayer have content. We have strong motives for perseverance. We have a growing though obscure knowledge of the Father before whom we are trustfully exposed. We can recognize him as he comes to us in our daily lives, quickly discern his demands and with ever-growing depth and clarity. We have his own vision by which to interpret the revelation of material creation and human history.

Jesus draws us to himself not for himself but so as to take us to the Father. The Father has asked him to be our friend. He has confided us to him as a cherished possession and Jesus considers us more precious than the whole world and his own life. Jesus was unimportant to himself. We are only his friends in truth if we allow him to share his Father with us. Friendship with him entails absolute loyalty on both sides. He, most readily, most devotedly, lays down his life for his friends. On the other hand, his friends never let him down. They are at his side in all his trials, never desert him whatever happens. They stand up before 'men' and acknowledge him, never allowing the opinions, fashions, ridicule or persecutions of 'men' to lead them to betray or deny their friend. And when we are his friends, how confidingly we can approach the Father.

Jesus teaches his friends a prayer that enshrines all he wants to teach them, all he asks of them. It is addressed to *Abba*. We are to say 'Our Father.' We know he is Father, not because we have proof or because, in the course of our lives, we detect a fatherly care, or because we often feel a warm loving presence, or because we see him granting our little wishes. No, we acknowledge him as Father for none of these reasons but simply because Jesus guarantees him. As with Jesus himself, everything can seem contrary to what we normally mean by father-love and care. By staking everything on Jesus' guarantee and trying to live always in the faith that God is Father, we come to know what he is: that he is our ground and air, that he is our encompassing and the source of what we are and do. If we reflect carefully we shall find that we catch ourselves out in attitudes, words, actions, doubts, fears, scruples that belie our notional belief. In actual fact, if not in professed belief, we assume that he is difficult to approach, that he is not concerned with us and has to be won over onto our side.

A friend told me recently of a little girl who was afraid when she woke up alone at night and frequently disturbed her parents by going along to them. 'But you are not alone,' the mother reassured her, 'Jesus is with you.' 'I know,' her daughter replied, 'but I want someone with skin on.' This heartfelt, vivid declaration echoes our own yearning. We find it so hard to live by faith alone, as we say. We too want someone 'with skin on.' The danger is that we try to put skin on. Misleading things are often said and written about the development of prayer and, probably, the outpourings of the mystics have been frequently misinterpreted. Certainly one picks up the idea that sooner or later we shall realize the presence and love of God almost as though it were on the same level and mode of perception as human love. This is to overlook that our *Abba* is 'in heaven.' These are Jesus' words. *Abba* though he is, he is completely other, transcendent mystery. Between him and us there lies an unbridgeable gulf that we could never cross. He himself has thrown the bridge: his Jesus. Only because he has done this can we know him and the breath-taking truth that he calls us to intimacy. Our approach to him must always be with awe. 'O come, let us worship and bow down, let us kneel before the Lord, our maker!' Our whole being must be bowed in worship all day long. And we must renounce the desire to have a God we can handle. We can be like people at a seaside resort who prefer the man-made swimming pool with its easy temperature, safety and amenities. After all, it is sea-water! And a little beyond is the open sea, untrammelled, un-tameable, over which we have no control whatever. But it is to this sea that we must commit ourselves and let ourselves be carried away. It is terrifying, this immense sea that is God. What will he do with us? Where will he carry us? He is *Abba,* says Jesus. Fear not, trust him.

Faith is not a thing of the mind; it is not an intellectual certainty or a felt conviction of the heart. It is a sustained decision to take God with utter seriousness as the God of my life. It is to live out each hour in a practical, concrete affirmation that God is Father and he is 'in heaven'. It is a decision to shift the centre of our lives from ourselves to him, to forego self-interest and make his interests, his will our sole concern. This is what it means to hallow his name as Father in heaven. Often it may seem as if we only act 'as if', so unaffected are our hearts, perhaps even mocking us: 'where is your God!' It is this acting out 'as if' that is true faith. All that matters to faith is that God should have what he wants and we know that what he wants is always our own blessedness. His purposes are worked out, his will is mediated to us, in the humblest form, as humble as our daily bread.

It is perhaps not too difficult to see God's providence in certain areas of our lives but it is likely that hour follows hour, full of little events, decisions and choices that seem, in fact, to be divorced from him. If so we are denying him as *Abba.* We do not allow him to reign over us totally. We may even excuse ourselves under the illusion that in our case the requisite conditions for total loving are not present. 'It would be different if such and such were different. Our situation is far

21

too distracting and worrying.' The truth is devastatingly simple and we are tempted to shirk the stark, overwhelming reality that God is giving himself to us in the stream of the ordinary, mundane events of our ordinary, mundane life. This is where he is for us, here and not elsewhere. Here, precisely here, must we hallow his name. Nothing is wanting to us. 'Fresh and green are the pastures where he gives me repose.' It is not for us to judge whether they are in truth fresh and green and sustaining. If he puts us there, even though they seem to us barren and hard, a place of struggle rather than repose, they are the pastures we need and in which we shall grow. We pray 'Give us this day our daily bread.' When you pray, Jesus tells us, you have to believe your prayer is already heard. We cannot judge results. We are certain that everything that comes to us is our daily, nourishing bread. This is what it means to believe: to take that daily bread and eat it with love and gratitude no matter how bitter the taste. By nature we, as it were, stand on the viewpoint of self and judge other people, things, what is happening from that stand. Faith demands that we deliberately get off that stand and move to another, the viewpoint of Jesus, and then, how different everything looks. This needs constant effort, constant readjustment. Unless we undertake this battle against our subjectivity – how we feel, how things look to us and so forth – and choose to stand on Jesus and live our lives in his vision, we shall never get anywhere. And yet, how few do this day in day out until it is second nature, their own nature. These indeed, have put on the mind of Christ.

Jesus bids us say 'Our Father', and to hallow this Father's name must mean taking very seriously that everyone is his child and my brother or sister. 'As God's chosen ones, holy and beloved, we must put on compassion, kindness, lowliness, meekness and patience; forgiving one another...' We must show constant, unconditional love and goodness to all, no matter how they treat us, because this is what God is like and does. He is forgiveness: a love always on tiptoe to forgive. As soon as we are there to receive he gives himself. We, too, must be like this, we must respond to others like this. Unless we do so, we cannot receive God's love. We have turned away from him. Nowhere, except when he is quoting the *Shema*, does Jesus speak of our loving the Father. He tells us we must believe in the Father, trust him, obey him, and love our neighbour. It can seem presumptuous to speak of loving God – as though we could! We love Jesus and he has spelt out for us what loving him means: keeping his com-mandments. This surrender to Jesus in keeping his words, immediately puts us in the Father's waiting embrace. 'Those who love me will keep my word, and my Father will love them.' (Jn. 14.23) In these words a loving fellowship is established. Jesus loves the Father. The Father loves Jesus. Only in Jesus can we love the Father and receive his love. We love the brother or sister that we see, those who are living with us in our mortal life and, in doing so, we are loving the unspeakable mystery, the Father.

O righteous Father, the world has not known thee, but I have known thee; and these have known that thou has sent me. I have made known to them thy name and will make it known, that the love with which thou hast loved me may be in them, and I in them. (Jn. 17.25–6)

Sometimes we can feel as if life is just too hard, or just too uninteresting and drab. It can seem that the obstacles within ourselves are mountainous and insuperable. Jesus' own unwavering faith must be ours. 'Everything is possible to those who believe,' was his humble boast. When everything seemed to be going wrong for him, when the 'no' of human hearts had congealed into a hard rock that threatened to grind him down, he was certain that his Father could and would move that hard mass and drown it for ever. He died in hope, not in hopes realized. The picture of him asleep in the violent storm, when others were frantic, and angered by his seeming indifference, reveals his inmost heart in its perfect trust. If we would be his friends we must live like that. A friend of Jesus dares all and never says such and such is too hard. If God asks something then it is possible of accomplishment. Such a person evades nothing: be it trying situations, uncongenial people, difficult duties. They take each day as it comes with its pleasures and joys, its disagreeable things and pains, shouldering their cross and going with Jesus. The significance of the cross is not suffering but obedience: doing the Father's will regardless of whether it is easy or hard.

For true friends of Jesus, evil does not exist. Everything is turned to good. Death itself, the epitome of all that is evil and destructive, is transformed. In his wonderful riposte to the Sadducees, who denied the Resurrection, Jesus, himself still in faith and not in sight, gloriously affirms our everlasting future, simply because he knows his Father and he knows this Father could never abandon his friends. The idea is unthinkable. You are quite, quite wrong, he emphatically declares, and closes the issue.

Friends of God? Can it be? Yes. But there is only one way: by becoming 'son'; by accepting the friendship and companionship of Jesus so as to learn sonship from him and share in his sonship. In practice this means being utterly unimportant to ourselves, becoming selfless and empty, nothing but an echo – like Enoch who disappeared and was seen no more. This is the paradox: the one who has consented to be nothing but an emptiness for the Father's love, becomes (and only now, in this context of nothingness, dare we breathe the word) somehow 'equal' to God, raised up to be his friend, his beloved. 'The Father and I are one,' says Jesus. Lost in his *kenosis* the same can perhaps be said of us.

# CHAPTER THREE

# Faith, Trust, Surrender to God: This is Prayer

For Christians, those who claim Jesus as their Way, Truth and Life, the one who reveals the Godhead to us, through whom we are in God and God in us, prayer should be the simplest and most uncomplicated of activities. Yet this is not the impression given by numerous books on the subject, seminars held and the general, anxious search for ways of praying successfully. This fretfulness, this craving for techniques and skills relating to what, in fact, no one can teach, indicates a lack of faith. This should not surprise us. Faith is no easy matter. Jesus himself realized how hard it is for human beings really to believe. 'When the Son of Man comes, will he find faith on earth?' (Lk. 18.8) 'Who then can be saved?' the disciples exclaimed in a moment of rare illumination. Jesus looked at them and said, 'With God all things are possible.' (Mt. 19.25–6) This is the heart of our subject: that the essence of prayer is God. The God of Jesus, total Given-ness, is always there to love us and, in that loving, transforming and 'saving' of us, brings us to that perfect fulfilment for which we were created.

On our side prayer is simply being there: open, exposed, inviting God to do all God wants. Prayer is not *our* activity, *our* getting in touch with God, *our* coming to grips with or making ourselves desirable to God. We can do none of these things, nor do we need to, for God is there ready to do everything for us, loving us unconditionally. We all know this in theory; but how many really know it in terms of practical living? Implicitly, if not explicitly, we think we have to find our own way. Our truth, we assume, is identical with how it seems to *us*; what *we* think; *our* point of view. It is our own spiritual life we are wanting and our own prayer. Yet it is a statement of incontrovertible truth that 'I am the Way, and the Truth, and the Life; no one comes to the Father but by me.' (Jn. 14.6) The surest help we can give to ourselves and others is to exhort them to an ardent coming to grips with Jesus in the New Testament so as to 'get God right' and the constant plea for greater faith. Nothing else is needed.

Our particular focus here is on personal or solitary prayer, but a life that is truly Christian is all prayer. For God's 'chosen', life is an unceasing desire expressed in their practical choosing of the divine will in all that happens. It is a being there for God's coming in all the details of life, loving, purifying, transforming. Solitary prayer, liturgical prayer and the prayer of grace-filled activity are one and the same great work of God and our cooperation with it. All three are necessary; they are interdependent and nourish one another.

According to the Gospel of John, the only work the Father asks of us is to 'believe in the one whom he has sent.' (6.29) Do we believe? The more instructed we are, the more wary we must be of the gap between our theoretical knowledge and the attitudes that, in practice, direct our lives. We must be deeply concerned with closing this gap, checking our attitudes and actions against the truth that is Jesus. Anxiety about prayer, about our relationship with God, points to want of faith. We have not yet believed Jesus, who strains every nerve to convince us how utterly secure we are in the Father's fathomless love, who takes care of us with a solicitude that reaches down to minute details. The only wise thing is to abandon ourselves trustfully into God's hands. Until we pull ourselves out of our own spiritual lives, we only confuse and hinder. We need to cease our concern with our subjective reactions and stop our attempt to assess how we stand spiritually. If we really believe then we can let go of our frantic desire for some assurance from within ourselves, for some token, feeling or intimation that we think proves that all is well. We long to be perfectly sure.

Well, we cannot have that sort of sureness, for it is not to be had. But we already have absolute sureness: magnificent security in the *Abba* whom Jesus shows us. Sooner or later, each of us has to be confronted with the terrifying truth (or blissful truth, according to our faith) that we have nothing, nothing whatever, to go on or to rely on except

Jesus. In all other areas of life our own efforts and activity are crucial and we have to be thoroughly adult; but where the very heart of reality is concerned, where we stand *vis-à-vis* God, there we are only children. No other state is appropriate or possible. Our fears, complexities, scruples, complacency and conceit come from not fixing our eyes on him who is our way, our truth and our life. By nature, we tend to be fascinated by our own selves, even in our miseries. We dare not let go of this intense self-interest, feeling that if we do we will just dwindle into nothingness. We dread the void, dread the feeling of being spiritually inadequate. So we look around, in the name of prayer, for ways of diverting ourselves from simple, trusting exposure to Love. 'O foolish and slow of heart to believe' (Lk 24.25) that God is who God is! 'Master, I knew you to be a hard man, reaping where you did not sow, and gathering where you did not winnow.' (Mt. 24.25) Jesus knew the human heart and its pitiful caricature of God. No wonder we cannot trust that one! No wonder we shirk encounter!

Behind our confusion over prayer lies the assumption that, though God made us human, this same Creator expects something better of us than our humanity provides and is annoyed with our fumblings and spiritual helplessness. We fret to do something (we hardly know what) that in fact God doesn't want, or to achieve something God is not the least interested in. What we are doing in this is hiding, refusing to take the risk of trust. What of the actual practice of prayer? It should be clear now that our whole concern in whatever *we* do must have as its aim to hold us 'there' in faith before God. The first thing is to decide what time we will give to daily prayer and then remain stead-fastly faithful to it. This will be the primary proof of our seriousness. But prayer can never be just one activity in life. Prayer is a way of life and our whole day must be oriented to prayer. What is more, as the time of prayer draws near we must more con-sciously direct our thoughts and prepare for the time of the sacred tryst. Spiritual reading is another essential, and especially reading of Scripture: a little each day if possible and more when we have leisure. Fidelity to time, mental and psychological preparation, spiritual reading: these three activ-ities are our contribution, like the meagre bread and wine we bring to the Eucharist. We must also know what we are going to do to begin our period of prayer. It would be irresponsible merely to drift in, hoping something will just 'come'. At the same time, we must bear in mind that all we are trying to do is to help ourselves to be present for God to love us. We are not trying to achieve anything.

No one can maintain that one way of praying is better or higher than another. One will choose this method or device, another that. It is not valid to claim, for instance, that to move from quiet, reflective vocal prayer to using fewer words, or even no words at all, means we have climbed to a higher rung of the ladder and are closer to God. There is no ladder to climb; God has come down to us, God who comes most surely to the lowly, the poor, those who long for the Divine and who are not seeking for themselves in any way. Some may find they use the same method constantly, others may have no fixed way but change from day to day as their inclination directs. If we keep clearly before us the essence of prayer, if we truly want God, if we remain faithful to prayer and take the necessary trouble, there is nothing whatever to worry about, no matter how unsatisfactory our psychological experience of prayer. No guide is needed, for no one can teach us to pray. All anyone can do for others is bring them to the threshold of prayer but there, perforce, one must leave them. We cross the threshold of prayer in our unique solitariness. Above all, how we need to keep our eyes on Jesus! Apart from anything else, we could not otherwise persevere at it confronted, as we are, with incomprehensible Mystery. Here there is no hurricane, no earthquake, only 'silence complete'. (1 Kgs 19.12) Faith, trust, surrender to God: this is prayer.

All that is most important about us happens at a level below consciousness. So real prayer, prayer in its very essence, escapes our direct consciousness. Everything depends on our believing God is Love, utterly faithful, good and generous. Everything depends, too, on our handing ourselves over to God's loving designs, asking for no tangible certainties. Jesus, indeed, knew how demanding is this trust, and yet trust is the only way we can allow God to be completely good to us, according to God's own nature. 'He told them a parable, to the effect that they ought to go on praying and never lose heart.' (Lk. 18.1) The one who knows

32

the Father and who speaks to us from the depths of this knowledge assures us: 'God is hearing and answering you, his beloved. How could the Lover not do so! God is answering now, at this very moment. Only believe.' This is how God's kingdom comes on earth, through the 'elect, who cry out to him day and night' (Lk. 18.8) with longing hearts for the redemptive love of God to stream out to the world. When we reflect on our responsibility as those to whom it has been given to know God, surely we must feel shame at being so concerned for ourselves and our spiritual life. The truth that is Jesus will set us free from this futile self-preoccupation.

# CHAPTER FOUR

# Prayer that is Jesus

Prayer is not just one function in life, not even the most important function; it is life itself. We are truly alive, truly human, only when our whole life is prayer. Our understanding of what prayer is will depend on how we think of God. Perhaps we see God as a distant, almighty, albeit benevolent Being to whom we must, in duty bound, offer our worship, thanksgiving and petitions, coming before his throne at appropriate times to acknowledge his rights over us and to pay our dues. For the rest of the time we must get on with the business of living. Yes, we know God looks on and misses nothing. He is ready to reward us for our good actions and find fault with us for our bad. For every good thing we do we get a credit mark beside our names and the sum total of these credits or merits determines the sort of happiness we will have in heaven when we die.

Or we may understand that in reward for the good we do God gives us grace: a mysterious something that makes us strong and beautiful and pleasing in his sight. Adorned with this, when we die we shall be sure to be admitted to the wedding banquet of eternity. All this is a caricature, I know, but perhaps it is nearer to our *real*, as distinct from our merely intellectual conceptions, than we like to admit.

With such ideas of God and of how we stand in relation to him then, of course, prayer is only one function in life. It has little to do with who I am: my gross reality and the broad expanse of my life. How different the truth! And this we learn, not from our poor, sin-blinded, self-centred hearts, but from Jesus, who alone reveals to us what the Father, our own dear God, is like.

This God is not 'out there' but most intimately present to me, in the blood pulse of my life. He is not a great Lord taking delight in the homage of his vassals and affronted when it is withheld. He isn't interested in himself at all but only in us. Our happiness is his happiness. We are his obsession; he is engrossed with everything that concerns us, every detail of our lives, every cell of our bodies. All is matter for his passionate concern. Jesus tells us so. He has all the anxious, tender, cherishing love of the best of parents. This simple statement of God's love for each of us is too overwhelming for us to master. Most of the time we must accept it 'in faith', as we say. What matters is not our savouring it in mind and emotion but our living by it.

God's one desire and purpose is to give himself to me ... What can this mean for my sense-dependent nature? Again, it must be held in dark faith: to have God thus is my blessedness and, until it is fact, until I am wholly possessed by him, I remain unhappy and unfulfilled. I have received human expression of the love of the Father through my brother, Jesus, a 'man like us'. Without him I could not know it and could never persevere in holding on to this knowledge were it not for him whose very essence is to be surrendered to, and possessed by, God. And this, precisely, is what prayer is.

Our mortal span in God's eyes is the opportunity for us to be prepared to receive God. It is an opportunity for God to come close to us. And this 'coming close' is to prepare us for total presence and indwelling. Never does the initiative lie with us. We haven't to persuade God to be good to us but have only to surrender to the goodness that surrounds us.

No one can come to the Father except through Jesus. This solemn affirmation has untold implications. It does not necessarily imply that I must always have an explicit advertence to Jesus when I come to pray, or that I must consciously direct my prayer through him, though, for a Christian, this will always be the normal way. What it means is that I, of myself, cannot attain God. Now, human pride believes it can. Intellectually we know better, but in practice most of us assume that we must 'do it ourselves'. Religious people, on the whole, think that by generous ascetic and spiritual effort they can come eventually to an experience of union with God. This is not so. Only One has attained the Father and we can attain him only insofar as we allow ourselves to be caught up in Jesus, carried along by him. In practice this means renouncing any spiritual achievement we have or want to have. It means disregarding what we feel or don't feel. It means seeking God for himself alone, not for anything that we can get out of it.

To acknowledge that we have absolute need of the mediator, Jesus, means a practical acceptance of the fact that, to attain to God, we must die with Jesus: not of ourselves, or by ourselves, but 'in him'. I must enter into his death. This death is a death to my self-centredness and self-possession. It is an ecstasy: a going right out of myself to belong to God. This is the essence of faith. I cannot achieve it myself; it is wrought by God and is the effect of mystical contact. God reveals himself to the inmost depths of the self, but 'no one can see God and live.' However, God can never come to us in this way until we have done all we possibly can to prepare for him. We must go to our limits, helped by his ordinary grace. Only when we have come to the end of what we can do is he able to step in with a direct, unmediated communication.

This preparation consists in doing everything I can to get to know about God, that is: searching for him with my mind. It consists in trying to know his will and devoting myself utterly to it. It also demands great fidelity to prayer, regardless of suffering and difficulties. This last point is of the greatest importance, because for God to 'touch' me, however lightly, means I suffer. I begin to shrivel up, to experience something of my sinfulness and total helplessness. I will come to realise with poignant intensity that I know nothing about God, that to me he has not yet revealed his name. I had thought I was spiritual, contemplative even; and now I see that I am an empty husk. What is more, I know that I can never know him and never come to him. It is then that I really experience that I need Jesus and everything depends on my living this out, letting go of the controls, handing them over to him and accepting to have no holiness, no achievement of my own, to be before God as nothing. This is to die so that Jesus becomes my all.

Contemplation has nothing whatever to do with states of feeling, what we experience or don't experience at prayer. It is not an achievement. It has nothing whatever to do with me except that I receive it. It is absolutely God's work, his taking possession of me. Ultimately, to be a contemplative means to be holy, to be transformed into Jesus. But let us make no mistake. This profound communication of God cannot be known by our natural faculties. Yet it seems that very few grasp this. There is talk of experiences deeper than emotion, of a refined spiritual awareness that is, at least, a token of God's communication. But everything of this kind is, at bottom, sense experience, no matter how refined and spiritual it seems to be. The ecstatic experience of self – the aim of some natural religions – is still a merely natural thing and has nothing in common with what is under discussion here. God's direct communication and his transforming action *must* remain secret. Only by their fruits will they be known: by a quality of life.

It is only too easy for spiritual persons to be more concerned with 'contemplative experience', with a 'spiritual life', with prayer as an art or technique producing various states of emotion, than with God. True prayer is selfless, whereas this sort of thing is self-seeking, a self-culture of the most flattering kind. Without a very exceptional grace at the outset we cannot seek God on our own. There is an enormous amount of self in what we think is our search for God, but God sets to work to purify this and we must accept this purification, which is painful because it strikes at our most cherished possession – our spiritual achievement.

The Mass is the supreme expression of prayer because it holds, for me, at this moment, the mystery of Jesus himself in his surrender to the Father and in the Father's response to that surrender. Here we see that it is God who does everything. I can only be there, saying my *fiat* and surrendering with Jesus. This is the pattern of all true prayer. Once we have really grasped this, prayer is simple indeed – so simple that it can easily scandalize because it isn't sublime or exalted enough! It is simple but it isn't easy, just because it is sacrifice and surrender, and these are never easy. It is life lived out for God alone.

Jesus takes it for granted that his disciples will set aside time exclusively to communing with God. This was his practice and he expects it of us. It follows the logic of love. I have a Father who loves me to folly; I want to be with him. Jesus knew this prayer would not be easy and that it would be hard to persevere. What is happening is secret not only to others but to ourselves as well. Only One is going to get any satisfaction out of it and his reward will be for something that costs us. Our satisfaction is solely that of giving God joy.

Once we have grasped the true nature of prayer we won't need a lot of instruction about how to comport ourselves. There are no techniques to learn. If we are wanting God and not ourselves there will be no problem at all; I will always know what to do and never be upset or thrown by what I feel or don't feel. Asking nothing for myself – no feedback, no assurances beyond what Jesus himself has promised – I will persevere through thick and thin. He has said that if I ask I will receive; that if I seek I will find; and that, when I knock, the door is opened. I believe him. I am sure that all is well, that God is doing everything for me, that Jesus is praying in me. I don't ask to see the gift in my hand, to feel that I have passed through the open door and received the bliss of his embrace. All my concern is that God should have what he wants: the chance to be good to me to his heart's content. And this surpasses all my understanding. I have staked my all on the God who never disappoints.

# CHAPTER FIVE

# 'If you knew the gift of God...'

*Who has believed what we have heard?*
*And to whom has the power of the Lord been revealed?*
                                                        Isa. 53.1

The Evangelist John takes up these words of Isaiah and applies them directly to Jesus: the incredulity, the blindness of human beings that characterize the biblical story of God's dealings with men and women in the Old Testament, reach their climax in the failure, the refusal, to recognize in Jesus the Messiah of God and, more than the Messiah, the very Son of the God they acknowledged as their God. (Jn 12.38)

Privileged as we are, it is all too easy for us Christians to take our faith for granted, confident that we do believe, do 'have' faith and in this comfortable assurance, not allow ourselves to be challenged by the likelihood of there being large areas of non-faith. 'We believe in God,' we affirm Sunday after Sunday. What do we mean? What does the word 'God' mean to us? Describe your

'God'. How do you know this 'God' of yours really is? When you think about it carefully, from where does your idea or understanding of God come?

Now, the New Testament proclaims – it is the good news it bears – that 'God', however we might conceive of 'God' (and inevitably the human heart, consciously or unconsciously, forms some idea of God to affirm or deny), can be known only through Jesus Christ and Jesus Christ as crucified. This is the revelation that stuns merely human wisdom and all those ideas of God that derive from the human mind and heart. It is the revelation of the divine that to the Jews was an obstacle they could not surmount, a scandal pure and simple, and to the pagans was ludicrous folly. Jesus of Nazareth, in his unprotected, raw human-ness, in his weak and suffering flesh and, supremely, in his terrible Passion and death, is clean contrary to human ideas of the divine. (1 Cor. 1.22–4)

This may seem a startling affirmation. What about the Resurrection? Jesus' earthly life, his Passion and death, belong to the past. Surely it is the glorious, risen Christ with whom we have to do, and it is this glorious One who is the image of God? Undoubtedly. But what can we see of this Risen One? As Luke tells us clearly, the holy cloud of the divine Mystery took him from human sight. (Acts 1.9) We know the heart of the Risen One, how he is to us, what he does for and in us, precisely through his earthly life and in his Passion and death. The Risen One, 'at the right hand of the Father', is Jesus and none other. We know that within the very heart of the Trinity, in 'heaven', there is that same passion of love for us, that same Self-expending outreach, that 'nothing spared', that sheer excess of love which, in the reality of this world and ourselves as we are, found its most expressive form in the denuded, dispossessed man on the gibbet.

This is the Christian God, the living God, the God who really is. This is the God whom Jesus called Father, whose image he is, and who must be surrendered to or denied. What of ourselves? If we examine our ideas, and the attitudes which flow from these ideas, do we not uncover assumptions regarding the Godhead that derive from human wisdom and that we have transposed onto Jesus and, from him, onto Jesus' God and Father? We can and perhaps do create a Jesus in the image and likeness of God but it is a God of our human conception. This will always be our natural tendency. We fail to know him even as the Jews of old failed to 'see' Jesus or recognize who he is. Progressively, painfully, with many a backward slither, each and every one of Jesus' followers has to allow Jesus – his person, his life, his death and his Resurrection – to correct, perhaps even to destroy and then reshape, their understanding of God. Theoretical knowledge is not enough. We suffer from the same inbuilt blindness and resistance to recognition as they did. Possibly it is Paul who expresses most dramatically this radical collapse of God, the God he had served with zeal and passion. We see him literally thrown to the ground and blinded by the vision – of what? The unbelievable! The crucified Jesus as the very wisdom and power of God! (Acts 9.1–9; 22.6–11; Gal. 1.15–16) Such a revelation can come only from God. Paul was sure of this; it was none other than God Himself who revealed His Son. Such knowledge as this transcends human wisdom. It is 'what eye has not seen, nor ear heard.' (1 Cor. 2.9)

If we want to know God, Reality, Bedrock and Ground, Absolute Origin, ineffable Mystery, that in which we and all that is exist as tiny fish in an infinite ocean, we must look at Jesus crucified. Holding up the cross, bidding us gaze into that bleeding, humiliated face, the Holy Spirit's focus is not first and foremost on suffering, or even on sin and its consequences, but on a love that is absolute, 'out of this world', 'other', 'what no eye has seen, nor ear heard, nor the human heart conceived.' We must gaze and gaze with fullest attention and then affirm: this is God; this is what God is really like. Through this vision we have the certainty of what is beyond our comprehension, that God is love and nothing but love, and that he is love to and for us. It is not enough merely to affirm God's loving interest and care – one need not be a Christian to hold that sincerely. What we see in Jesus is a Self-gift on God's part that is the fullest content of love. God gives not gifts but God's own Self:

> 'Our soul is so preciously loved of Him that is highest that it passeth the knowing of all creatures. That is to say that there is no creature that is made that may fully know how much, how sweetly and how tenderly that our Maker loveth us.'
>
> (Julian of Norwich, *Revelations of Divine Love*)

Any notion whatsoever that sets a figure of divine wrath over against Jesus, who not only demands just retribution for human iniquity but demands it of Jesus in our stead, a Father who imposes an appalling sacrifice on the Son while He Himself remains aloof, untouched, in the realms of the divine, can only be considered blasphemous by us today, whatever its pedagogical value to former generations. It is the Evangelist John who shows us clearly the communion of life, heart and will between Father and Son. It is the Father's excess of love for us that, in filling the heart of Jesus, drives Jesus to his self-emptying. In keeping nothing back from us, loving us to the uttermost, giving us his all, we know that it is the Father living in him who is keeping nothing back from us and giving us His all. In giving us Jesus He gives us His all.

The principle labour of the Christian is to believe that divine love is the breadth and length and height and depth, and that there is simply nothing above, below or beyond it. It is our home; it enfolds us and is our utmost security both in this life and in death and beyond. We are speaking of faith, not of feelings or intellectual grasp. For faith means a blind trust in and surrender to the God of love and this love is too great for our human heart and mind. We are to live life no longer as our own, relying on our own pathetic vision of reality and of how God is to us, but clinging, mind and heart, to the Son of God who 'loved me and sacrificed himself for me.'(Gal. 2.20) We must train ourselves to renounce our natural mode of seeing and evaluating. This must be at the service of faith, yet must not be taken for faith. Without realizing it, we can call 'faith' that assent we give to our own manageable ideas of God. True faith takes us into the unknown. It calls for blind trust; it calls for profound humility and surrender. This is real asceticism, the self-denial that Jesus tells us is essential if we are to be his disciples.

If the heart of Christianity is the God who gives nothing less than God's own Self, it follows, as a logical conclusion, that the fundamental stance a Christian must take is that of receiving Him. First and foremost we must accept to be loved, allow God to love us, let God be the doer, the giver, let God be God to us. But how hard it is for us to do that consistently! We are always reversing the role, intent on serving God, as we say, on doing things for God, offering God something. This is our natural bent, but it must be corrected by the vision of faith. Over and over again, Jesus tries to get his disciples to drop this self-important attitude and to understand that, before God, they are only very small children who have no resources within themselves, but must look to their parents for everything, simply everything. It is not their role to give, but to receive. Jesus knows that this calls for a radical change of outlook and, more than outlook, a radical change of heart. From always trying to prove ourselves to God (is it not really to ourselves?), we have to become poor in spirit just as Jesus was. Jesus remained always a small child before his Father, always poor and dispossessed. The one thing in himself to which he draws attention is his meek and humble heart. How

48

vividly John shows us the poverty of Jesus living only by the Father, disclaiming any life of his own, any personal resource. He is an emptiness into which the Father is always flowing, an unwritten melody waiting for Him to sing.

There are countless incidents in the Gospel narratives, not to speak of the letters of Paul, John and the Letter to the Hebrews, that challenge us to this change of heart. We find it so hard a lesson to learn! Luke's little story of Jesus in Martha's house (Lk. 10.38–42) illustrates the point vividly. Martha, having welcomed her guest, does the obvious, expected thing and prepares a meal for him. Instead of helping her, Mary, her sister, sits down at the Lord's feet and listens to him. Martha is cross with Mary and still more cross with Jesus for allowing her to remain idle while she, Martha, bears the brunt of work. Instead of chiding Mary, Jesus, albeit very gently, chides the busy, well-meaning Martha. He defends Mary for doing the right thing, choosing the better part. Luke is using this incident to stress the point that, in the presence of Jesus – no ordinary guest – the only proper thing to do is to allow him to feed us, to serve us. This is the only service he wants from us. Similarly, Peter, although he had long been in intimate relationship with Jesus, still found the lesson hard to learn and remonstrated with Jesus who was kneeling before him to wash his feet (Jn 13.6–8). Jesus insisted that it must be so; if Peter wanted to be Jesus' disciple he had to accept the fact that Jesus (and that means God) is our servant. Jesus makes it clear that he does not like his true disciples to think of themselves as servants of God. They are to see themselves as beloved, as friends, as familiars in His company. However this means sharing Jesus' own vision, his knowledge of his Father, which must radically change their whole outlook. Then they will glimpse, with awe, with trembling gratitude, something of the divine Self-abasement in pure love to us. It is out of depths of humility and love, ever aware of being served by divine love, that the disciple turns to serve others. 'Do as I have done', Jesus says. (c.f. Jn 13.13–17)

For me, it is not without significance that Luke relates the Martha and Mary story immediately after the parable of the Good Samaritan. (Lk. 10.29–37) We can see that the Samaritan, consciously or not, was listening to God, looking at God and therefore recognized Him immediately in the wounded man and set to work to minister to Him, for we minister to God, serve God, only in our neighbour. The priest and Levite were, like Martha, intent on serving God. Presumably they were hastening on their way to the Temple to perform their respective religious duties. Seeing the stricken figure they may well have thought it a corpse, contact with which would involve a ritual uncleanness that would prevent them from carrying out these duties. They pass by. Each of us must be Martha and Mary at one and the same time. Only if we have the heart of a Mary will our service of others be selfless. Not only the service of our neighbour, but what we call our religious practices, will be shot through with self-seeking unless we are always little children at our inmost centre, expecting God to be utterly good to us.

It is well, for instance, to check our motives in regard to our celebration of the Eucharist and the other sacraments. Do we see going to Mass or going to Confession merely as religious duties, obligations imposed on us? Why, really, do I go to Mass? Why do I go to Confession? Would I be afraid not to go? And if so, of what? Do we have an anxiety about our Confession? What we have to understand is that in the sacraments Jesus comes to us immediately, directly, to heal and transform us and bring us into full union with himself and his Father. We receive the sacraments, not to give something to God, but to allow God to do and to become everything to us. How simple this ritual! What more simple and true than to hold out an empty hand to receive the fullness of life? What more simple if, having admitted our lack of love and the meanness of our response to love, admitted that, even if we are as yet too blind to see them, there are within us great areas of non-faith and non-love, to then hear the voice of the Son of God through the Church calling us to life and freedom. (c.f. Jn 5.25) (For, 'absolve him' is, I believe, the same expression Jesus used when he commanded the community present at his summoning Lazarus from the tomb to unbind his friend's imprisoned limbs (Jn 11.44).)

Again: maybe we have undertaken some Lenten penance. What is our motive? Is it because a good Catholic always does something for Lent? Do we assume that penance is a good thing, that God is pleased when we do hard things for Him? All this hardly fits the God Jesus shows us. Yet what God longs for us to do is to live in the truth Jesus reveals. This means believing in God's absolute, unconditional love, not in a notional way but one that transforms our attitudes and whole approach to life. We cannot hope for this real knowledge without effort on our part. 'Think,' says John, 'think of the love the Father has for us ...' (1 Jn 3.1) What can be more important for a disciple than constantly to reflect on the truth of God, on this unspeakable, incredible love with which we are encompassed? But how often do we do so?

In the light of all this, surely we see that no Christian may dispense with prayer. And maybe, too, we have to change the whole conception of prayer that sees it as a time, short or long, when, so to speak, we have to entertain God with holy thoughts or worthy sentiments and words. When we feel that our performance is hopeless, we get discouraged and conclude that, whatever the general truth about the needfulness of prayer, for us at any rate, no doubt because of our inadequacy, it is a waste of time and we had better do something really useful for God. Once again, we are forgetting the truth that God is the doer and giver. Christian prayer is nothing other than being present to God so that God can give to us. The only thing that matters is that we believe this and stay there with Him, regardless of how we feel or don't feel. I suggest that the most profound expression we can give to faith is to set aside an inviolable time each day, no matter how short, when we deliberately affirm God's, Jesus' absolute love for me here and now and that we stay there in blind trusting faith, receiving it. This will mean learning the precious lesson that, in fact, we have no inner resources of our own; it will mean learning to live happily without any assurances from within ourselves but casting our whole weight on to infinite love. This is to glorify God for it glorifies God's true nature, which is love.

If we knew the gift of God ... 'Lord, that I may really see! That I may really listen! I do believe, but, oh Lord, help the areas of unbelief!'

CHAPTER SIX

# Prayer in the Trinity

Karl Rahner, writing some years ago, made the obser-
vation that the majority of Catholics are Unitarians,
in that as far as their conscious experience goes, the
mystery of the Holy Trinity is merely a dogma and
a totally baffling one at that: an 'article of faith' to
which, as good Catholics, they ascribe but which
seems to have no relationship to life. I have difficulty
in accepting this criticism. Surely, to believe in Jesus
Christ implies some sort of experience or awareness
of the Trinity in relation to ourselves? *The* Christian
prayer, the Our Father, the Lord's (Jesus') prayer:
'Pray like this: "Our Father ..."' (Mt. 6.9) inescapably
confronts us with a Twosome. St Teresa of Avila,
introducing a Sister to the practice of mental prayer,
as she would call it, shows her how to recite the Our
Father in such a way that is she is praying mentally:

> '...my daughter, as you are alone, you must look for a
> companion – and who could be a better Companion
> then the very Master Who taught you the prayer you are
> about to say?'
>
> (St Teresa of Avila, *Way of Perfection*, ch. 26)

And further on: '... for however much your thoughts may wander, between such a Son and such a Father there must needs be the Holy Spirit.' (ch. 27) It seems to me that what is missing to our consciousness is not experience but lack of reflection, whereas St Teresa excelled in reflecting on her experience. Today the Church enjoys a vibrant liturgical life and Catholics are exposed to the riches of liturgical texts in their own language; texts that are, of course, wholly Trinitarian. It is possible that Rahner's stricture referred to a time preceding this reform and, hopefully, it no longer pertains. Still, I think an enormous amount is to be gained from reflection on our own experience and this is what I intend to do here.

Having agreed to write on the life of the Father, Son and Holy Spirit in prayer by 'drawing on personal experience' forces me to examine carefully what the Trinity *actually* means to me, not what I think it *ought* to mean (always a temptation because it is a safe evasion). To the questions implicitly (and often explicitly) raised: 'Does the mystery of the Holy Trinity affect your prayer? Would your prayer be any different abstracting from it?' My immediate and unhesitating answer would be that, without the mystery of the Trinity, I would have no prayer. I simply cannot imagine praying to a monad, a Great Alone. What would I be doing, a tiny consciousness like mine, looking into nothingness, just hoping that something, or someone, is there but with no certainty whatsoever? And if I took the risk of saying 'Yes, there is Something', even a 'Someone', what then?

What does it do for me? Where does it lead me? How is this 'Whatever-it-is' related to me? Even the attempt to express the hypothesis seems absurd. I affirm that with no Trinity, prayer would not make sense to me. So I have to try to explain that, even to myself, because I don't suppose that, objectively speaking, it is obvious.

I was born into and brought up in a Catholic home and community and therefore the names 'Father', 'Son', 'Holy Spirit' were constantly on my lips. Did they mean anything? Hard to say. I always realized that Jesus was not Father; that when we prayed 'Our Father' we did not mean Jesus but 'God the Father.' The familiar figure was, of course, Jesus – as the Sacred Heart, the Good Shepherd, the Infant of Bethlehem. What is more, I knew that Jesus was God, that I adored him in the Blessed Sacrament and could pray to him. The Mass in those far off days was in Latin. Our parents always followed the Mass from an English Missal and, as soon as we were old enough, we were taught to do the same, so, in this way, I knew that it was the sacrifice of Jesus offered to God. At school we invoked the Holy Spirit for help in our studies; the school year opened with the Mass of the Holy Spirit, and there was, of course, the feast of Whitsunday. Some idea of Trinity was there from the start, but I cannot say that, consciously, it made any impression on me. When I was sixteen my inmost depths were smitten by a 'realization' of the reality of God. There is nothing to be said of that 'moment' other than that it turned me upside down. I knew that *there* was the only Answer for me; life had no meaning except that Unutterable. Looking back, I think I could say that I was faced with a real puzzle. I knew that that mysterious, hidden, silent One was the answer – and the only answer – to the huge question mark, the nameless yearning that was I. Yet this One was inaccessible: there, but not, apparently, for me. Was I sure that God wanted *me?* Catholic Christian though I was, in actual, conscious experience I was faced with a Monad who had, nevertheless, 'bewitched' me. From where I stand now, in a wholly trinitarian context, I know it was the Holy Spirit who held me in the Catholic Church and fidelity to the sacraments. Yet I could not see the connection. The Church, the sacraments, doctrine, seemed incongruous, unconnected with that Absolute. Thoughts about Jesus and devotional practices could never satisfy me; they seemed far removed from that Something. This keen awareness, the sharp edge of 'realization', inevitably wore off but its powerful effect remains to this day. It took years before the apparent rift between the two experiences disappeared. It happened imperceptibly.

As a young Carmelite, I was constantly exposed to the Liturgy. I studied the prayers of the Mass and the texts for the Divine Office throughout the liturgical year. The only form of 'piety' that made any appeal to me was what I would now call biblical theology. I read and reread the Gospels; prayed and prayed the stories and dialogues, seeing myself always as the person Jesus was confronting, and begging Jesus for the same graces of cleansing and healing: for sight, living water, food, faith, love ...

I also prayed his own prayers: in the course of his ministry, at the last supper and in the garden, and, of course, these prayers were to the Father. Often, I used to think of those nights he spent alone praying to his Father, and wanted to identify myself with this prayer. I did all this as the most obvious response to what I was being shown and offered in the Gospel. I found similar incentives to pray in the words of Paul, John and others, turning their magnificent statements of theology into personal prayers; and I would beg with all my heart for the fulfilment in me of what these wonderful texts were revealing concerning God's incredible designs of love. I was aware that I was not a lone individual; to pray for myself in this way was to pray for everyone else. The New Testament became prayer. I realized that God spoke to me, revealed Himself to me in these texts, and my prayer was my response.

In this way, almost unconsciously, my prayer took a Trinitarian form. I knew that the lodestone of my being, inaccessible, utterly beyond the range of thought or feeling, had come to us and looked at us in pure friendliness and love through the eyes of Jesus. In Jesus the Inaccessible was accessible and very intimate, dwelling within. There was no need to climb to heaven, no need to strive for illumination. Useless, anyway. Through looking at Jesus, praying and trying to live the Gospel, I came to realize that the Inaccessible is absolute Love, and nothing but love. Love has come to us, is with us. God is not just 'God' but God is always 'God-with-us', 'God-for-us', 'God-who-has-us' in His heart. This is God; there is no other. It is not for us to raise irrelevant questions and indulge in speculations as to what God is in God's own self. I once tried to grapple with St Thomas Aquinas' treatise on the Trinity. It seemed to me brilliant speculation, not Truth; and it left me untouched. It was unusable where I was concerned, whereas I believe that all God has revealed to us is for use. The Truth I was looking for I found in the Gospel of John and Letters of Paul – particularly in the Letter to the Romans – and elsewhere in the New Testament, and in that Event which we know as the Passion, death, Resurrection and Ascension of Jesus and the sending of the Spirit. We know the Trinity as experience and only thus.

I think I am jumping ahead somewhat. It is very important for me to express how absolutely central and indispensable the human Jesus has become to me. In her famous treatise on prayer, *The Interior Castle*, St Teresa, in the fullness of her spiritual maturity and understanding of the ways of prayer, states emphatically that it is impossible to become truly holy, totally surrendered to God and transformed in God, except through conscious adherence to the Sacred Humanity of Jesus. (She is, of course addressing Christians.) If we would be wholly united to God, then we must take with practical seriousness that he is our only door into the divine Mystery: our Way, our Truth and our Life. I learned this through actual experience, finding myself utterly helpless, spiritually speaking. Having determined to give my life to prayer in the deepest meaning of that word, my expectations, vague though they were, were utterly shattered. I had no ability to pray; God remained utterly remote to me at the level of conscious experience. I had no sense of His presence, of being enfolded in love. Did I have any faith, I would ask myself. I could not claim that I had, that I could love either my neighbour or God if left to myself. If I had relied only on my merely human perception, how I felt things to be, I would have despaired and given up, telling myself it was all a great confidence trick! Or, if not that, then, at the least, that I myself was an abject failure and it was of no use to go on trying. But I didn't rely on myself; I took Jesus very seriously. I saw that my total helplessness was expressing a fundamental truth: we cannot save ourselves, cannot attain God, cannot cope with God, still less show off in His presence. To the bewildered disciples' question: 'Who then can be saved?' Jesus answered: 'It is impossible for humans but not for God. For everything is possible to God.'(Mk 10.27) Now I was experiencing this truth for myself. God has given us Jesus to be, as Paul tells us, 'our wisdom, our unhindered access to God, our holiness and our atonement.'(1 Cor. 1.30) So it doesn't matter when we feel our faith is very weak, hardly exists, or that we do not see, can't make sense of things: Jesus sees, Jesus knows and we are in Jesus. 'Christ is mine and all for me' says St John of the Cross. He is my wisdom, my faith, and his love is mine to love with. So we can afford to live with our poverty and, when we do so, it means that Jesus is *really* our only saviour – which is what he is for. I don't want the impossible task of saving myself, of producing, from any supposed resources of my own, a faith that moves mountains. I have come to understand that God has done it all for us in giving us Jesus. Our part is to *use* him to the uttermost. This taking Jesus for ourselves, or, conversely, living only in Jesus without any self-claim, is what it means to be 'in the Holy Spirit'. Identified with Jesus, we can afford to be very small, like 'little children' and, just like a confident, cherished child, we can take it for granted that our Father will do everything for us. In the Divine Office for the feast of the Immaculate Conception, there is a lovely antiphon which, broadly translated, reads:

> The Lord has clothed me head to foot in his redemption, thrown around me the cloak of His love, and made me holy.

Provided we try to do God's will in all things (which means, essentially, that we love others 'as I have loved you', with a self-sacrificing love), and provided we trust blindly in God-All-Love, each one of us can make this humble boast our own.

So far I have concentrated on the love of the Father for the Son and the Son's love for the Father and our entrance into that exchange of love. Does this make me open to the oft-heard criticism that the Holy Spirit is thereby overlooked? I would find such criticism absurd. 'Between such a Son and such a Father, there must needs be the Holy Spirit,' wrote St Teresa in the *Way of Perfection*. Of course, there must! But I am reflecting on *experience*, not theologizing, and my personal experience is, I believe, the experience of everyone who really has faith in Jesus and lives that faith: a gradual enlightenment, insight into scripture and dialogue between the Word and self.

It might seem that all this is only a human activity: a human person addressing the Son, Jesus, and, with him, addressing the Father. And so it is. But, if we look closely, we see clearly that this 'activity' simply cannot derive merely from ourselves. Often enough, it runs clean counter to natural perception, to what our senses tell us. Flesh and blood do not reveal these things, nor enable us to respond. There is a force, a Spirit within, that prompts, urges, enables us to ignore our own natural estimation of how things stand, and choose, instead, to believe. Nothing runs so counter to nature as the experience of our spiritual poverty, and a practical love for it such as this can only be the work of the Holy Spirit, the Spirit of Jesus. Do we not recognize the truth of Scripture that, in spite of everything that is 'against us', we are grounded in an invincible hope 'because the love of God has been poured into our hearts by the Holy Spirit who has been given to us.' (Rom. 5.5) We are being led, not by nature, but by the Spirit, for we are indeed God's children and the Spirit inspires our own spirit to cry out in confidence: 'Father, my dear Father' (c.f. Rom. 8.14–16). It is the Spirit who continually upholds our natural weakness with divine strength; who is always praying deep within us even when our hearts seem mute, uttering our own most authentic desires, desires that we hardly know we have.

These are Jesus' desires, formed and uttered in us as our very own by the Holy Spirit, the mutual Love-Exchange of Father and Son. Such prayer is infallibly heard (c.f. Rom. 8.26). I am sure we are not meant to peer into the Spirit's face, so to speak – nor can we do so any more than we can turn around and peer into our own. Jesus' is the face that we gaze on without ceasing and it is this face that the Spirit unveils to us. 'He will bear witness to me' (Jn 15.26) and 'He will lead you into all the truth.' (Jn 16.12) The Holy Spirit, who proceeds from the Father and yet is sent to us by Jesus himself, is nothing less than the love between the Father and the Son, their 'communion'. Our prayer can seem to us such a poor thing, so unsuccessful! We do not see the reality. Our prayer is one with that communion of love between Jesus and his Father which *is* the Holy Spirit.

Through the giving of the Beloved Son to the world (who is all God has to give, for God holds nothing back from us), and through that Son's love to the utmost, to total self-emptying, identifying with us in the whole range of our mortal life from conception to death; through the Father's having lifted him out of death into His own eternal life, endowing him with 'the glory which I had with You before the world began,' (Jn 17.5) we have come to know that Absolute Reality is love, a dynamic holy communion between Persons. We cannot 'sort it out', make a pattern of it: we can only surmise how it is and experience and live with the glorious consequences. 'The life of God is not something which belongs to God alone,' writes

Catherine Mowry LaCugna.

> 'Trinitarian life is also our life ... There is *one* life of the
> Triune God, a life in which we graciously have been
> included as partners ... a comprehensive plan of God
> reaching from creation to consummation, in which
> God and all creatures are destined to exist together in
> the mystery of love and communion.'
>
> (Catherine Mowry LaCugna, *God For Us*)

Jesus prays that we may be with him where he is in
the Father's heart, loved as he is loved: 'that they all
may be one; even as you, Father, are in me and I in
you ... The glory which you have given to me I have
given to them, that they may be one even as we are
one.' (c.f. Jn 17) Surely it is fitting to give time in
prayer to appreciating, realizing and deepening our
insertion into this communion of love?

CHAPTER SEVEN

# Amen: The Human Response to God

'I do as the Father has commanded me so that the world may believe that I love the Father.' (Jn 14.31) A little earlier in the same Gospel, Jesus has declared himself the Way, the Truth and the Life. Later he makes confession before Pilate that what he was born for, what he came into the world for, was to bear witness to the truth. The truth to which he bears witness is his love for the Father, expressed in absolute obedience and self-surrender unto death. It is John's Gospel that makes clear what is implicit in the synoptics: Jesus lives in total submission to his Father, his eyes always on Him, his ears constantly intent to listen. The Father is his life, his all. His unswerving obedience is joyous, the expression of an overwhelming love, a love so absolute that self-interest of any kind whatsoever disappears, and all that matters is the Beloved, the Beloved's concerns and longings – that He be hallowed in every human heart, that His kingdom come, that His will be done. Jesus' initiative consists solely in an unbroken waiting on the Father to discern His will, whether it be through events, through Scripture, through the voices of others (for example, his mother at Cana, or the Syro-Phoenician woman), or through the promptings of his own heart. His entire life consists in doing the Father's will in joyful surrender.

The famous hymn in Philippians 2 gives us evidence of how, at a very early date, Christians grasped that obedience was the mode of Jesus' being. Paul employs an older text to indicate that we must have the same mind as Christ. For Paul, Jesus' obedience unto death *is* our redemption: it has enabled the Father to raise, by the Spirit's power, him who had sunk for our sake to the lowest depths, and to constitute him a life-giving Spirit. What else but Jesus' never failing 'yes' to the Father is that 'powerful word' which 'sustains all things' (Heb. 1.3)? Both Hebrews and the Synoptic Gospels give us vivid insight into the cost of this willing, joyful obedience. We are shown Jesus weeping, crying out in pain and fear as he struggles agonizingly to accept what lies before him. The terrible evil perpetrated against him, the basest elements in human nature employed to torment, humiliate, degrade and destroy him, become 'the chalice which my Father gives me', a chalice to be drained to the dregs, drained with all the love of his heart.

Paul affirms:

> ... the Son of God, Jesus Christ, whom we proclaimed among you ... was not 'Yes' and No'; but in him it is

always 'Yes.' For in him every one of God's promises
is a 'Yes.' (2 Cor. 1.19–20)

The truth revealed in Jesus, expressed in his own
self-expending love, is the Father's incomprehensible, 'foolish' love for us. 'Passionate' is the word
we must use, for it is a love that stops at nothing,
pouring itself out in limitless self-abandon – a love
that is pure compassion, stooping down to raise us
up, a love enabling us to receive the divine embrace
of perfect union and respond to it. 'For this I was
born, and for this I came into the world, to testify
to the truth.' (Jn 18.37) In Jesus, we see the true
face of the Father, and the truth of humanity. 'Here
is the man!' (Jn 19.5) The only real life, for us as
for Jesus, is the Father's love. In and through Jesus,
the Father fulfils His will, His love for humanity.
The New Testament writers strain every nerve to
communicate something of what God has ordained
for us from 'before the foundation of the world'
(Eph. 1.4), a fulfilment beyond human conception.
'What no eye has seen, nor ear heard, nor the
human heart conceived, what God has prepared for
those who love Him.' (1 Cor. 2.9)

In this one human life with its limited span – an
existence in the flesh, beset with weakness, subject
to temptation, to suffering of heart, mind and body,
an existence like ours in everything except sin – the
Father accomplished the world's redemption, the
gathering in of the whole creation to Himself for
its perfect blissful fulfilment. From 'the beginning',
co-incident with our creation, is the glorious, irrevocable divine promise. Jesus is 'the Word', the

eternal 'yes', Amen to the Father, and, in his humanity, the Amen to the promise. The Book of Revelation specifically declares him so: 'the Amen, the faithful and true witness, the origin of God's creation' (3.14), who is also the Omega (1.8). Here then is our meaning as human beings: to love the Father. And this must mean, as for Jesus, a life of total obedience, total dedication to the Father's will. But the Father's will is always, and only, our perfect happiness in His love. Only His love can make us happy; and therefore our love, our obedience to the vocation that He has given us, consists in our being willing receivers of His transforming, beatifying love: to be 'Amen' with Jesus, the perfectly obedient one.

Though they express it in very different ways, both John and Paul have an inspired vision of our oneness with Jesus. In John, the very love that the Father has for Jesus includes each one of us. All that the Father has given to Jesus, Jesus gives to us. We live by Jesus' life, just as the branches of a vine exist and are sustained by the sap of the vine-stock. Cut off from it, we are lifeless – helpless to take even one step towards the Father. We depend on Jesus and Jesus depends on the Father. He draws life from his Father; we draw that same life from Jesus. This union *is* redemption. To be in Jesus is to be at home in the Father's heart. What we have to do, our only way, is to cleave to Jesus as our absolute Saviour.

Paul declares that Christ Jesus became for us 'wisdom from God, and righteousness and sanctification and redemption.' (1 Cor. 1.30) All is in him and only in him. We are incorporated into him. All that Jesus has done has become ours; what he has inherited becomes our inheritance. *Conmortui, consepulti, conresurrecti* – we have died with him, we have been buried with him, we have risen with him, (c.f. Rom. 6.1–11). We are co-heirs with Christ, dwelling already in heaven, the heaven where Christ is – or, more truly, which Christ is. As in John's vision, we *now* have eternal life. Baptism expresses, concretizes, 'contains' this inexpressible truth. At baptism we proclaimed our 'Amen', at least through our sponsors, pledging ourselves to live out what we have in principle become. Properly understood, this is what the Christian life is: an ever deeper integration of the reality of baptism, a deeper penetration into the inheritance that is ours, a surrendering of ourselves to the Spirit to be 'conformed to the image' of God's Son. (Rom. 8.29) Through baptism we are incorporated into the Church, God's chosen means of holding us in His Son and endowing us with the 'riches of His grace' – riches which He 'lavishes' upon us in Christ Jesus. (Eph. 1.7–8)

Every human being, by the very fact of their being human, is already, by God's free gift, set in the Promised Land, a land flowing with milk and honey – and Jesus is that Promised Land. Our earthly existence is sacramental in context: the riches of Christ, the treasures of God's love are communicated to us through created things. 'How silently, how silently, the wondrous gift is given' – and given unceasingly. Jesus comes into all the events of life, in the sacred word of Scripture, in our prayer, and, supremely, in the sacraments proper. Secretly, through these means, the divine Spirit works within our inmost hearts, purifying and transforming them, and making us truly children of God, inheritors of Jesus' kingdom. This union with God, lived purely and fully, is what we call 'mystical'; it is simple, direct, but all-transformative.

The 'inflow of God into the soul,' to use St John of the Cross' definition of mystical theology (*Dark Night of the Soul*, 2.5.1), is offered to us in the sacraments at a depth we shall never plumb. In them, under created realities, we have direct contact with Christ in all his saving power. The Eucharist is the sacrament of Jesus' sacrifice, of his total, loving surrender to the Father, and of the Father's embrace of him in Resurrection. This divine 'exchange' becomes ours, and we are taken into the triune life of love. Our offerings, representing ourselves, become the sacrifice of Jesus. The whole meaning of our Christian existence lies in allowing God to effect this transformation. In a mysterious but real way, we are to become the reality and presence of Jesus in the world. We do not need to conceive our own worship, adoration, love and thanksgiving – how inadequate they would be. The Father has given them to us, for the Eucharist is a worship and a love that are wholly worthy: the worship and love of the Son.

Similarly, there is no need for us to find a way of atoning, of 'making up for our sins' and for those of others. How much self-inflicted pain has been offered to the Father in 'reparation', in 'making satisfaction for sin', as though the Father finds pleasure in seeing us suffer! No, God in person has taken on Himself the burden of reconciliation; He and He alone can 'put things right', can make it possible for the estranged world to find its rightful place in the divine heart. At-one-ment is already achieved. In the Father's eyes we hung on the Cross with Jesus; the sorrow and the love with which the heart of Jesus answered the Father's scorned love has been given to us as our sorrow, our love, and our atonement. Our sin-caused alienation from the Father has been overcome. The Father's love for us, surging through his human heart, drove Jesus to take upon himself the sins of the world. He alone knows the reality of the Father's passionate love, 'appreciates' it as we ourselves can never do; therefore he alone can measure the dreadfulness of its rejection. 'It is for your sake that I have borne reproach, that shame has covered my face.' (Ps. 69.7) Innocent though he was, he hung upon the Cross as a sinner, his heart broken with love and sorrow. Love is the only salve for wounded love. The Father reaches out to His tortured Son and lifts him up to glory. The definitive judgment on sin is made, a judgment of total forgiveness. Through him, with him, in him, we offer love for love and are caught up into the same embrace. All is done for us: *consummatum est* – 'it is finished.' (Jn 19.30) This we celebrate, 'lay hold' of in a wholly personal way, in the Sacrament of Reconciliation.

We find it hard to accept how involved God is with us, how vital we are – by His free choice – to

His complete happiness. Scripture encourages us to find our analogies in human images. We are adopted children. Consider a blissfully happy couple finding all they need in one another. For no other reason than generosity and the desire to share their happiness, they decide to adopt children as their own. From then on their life undergoes a profound change. Now they are vulnerable; their happiness is wrapped up in the welfare of the children; things can never be the same again. If the children choose to alienate themselves and start on the path to ruin, the couple are stricken. They will plead, humble themselves, make huge sacrifices, go out of themselves to get their loved ones to understand that the home is still their home, that the love they have been given is unchanging. This perhaps, gives us some insight into redemption. In a mystery we cannot fathom, God 'empties', 'loses' Himself, in bringing back to Himself His estranged, lost children. And this is all the Father wants. This is the only remedy for His wound. God is no longer pure God, but always God-with-humanity-in-His-heart.

How do we ensure that what in principle has been done for us becomes wholly actual in each one of us? Every earnest Christian can say with some truth: 'it is no longer I who live, but it is Christ who lives in me.' (Gal. 2.20) But can we dare to claim that this is true in the fullest sense? Why is it, John of the Cross asks, that so few attain to this high state? He is certain that God wills it for all: it is our Christian vocation. The fault lies with us. We are not prepared, John says, to take the trouble to do all that we possibly can to prepare for the Holy Spirit's sanctifying activity, nor are we ready to accept the inevitable difficulty and suffering that are its effects:

> ... this highest union cannot be wrought in a soul that is not fortified by trials and temptations, and purified by tribulations darknesses, and distress ...
> (St John of the Cross, *Living Flame of Love*, 2.25)

Too readily such expressions seem to let us off the hook. 'That sort of suffering belongs to very special souls, not to an ordinary person like myself.' Pure fallacy. The life of every one of us, as it unfolds day by day with its obligations, anxieties, demands – all the ups and downs of the 'ordinary' person – contains everything that the Holy Spirit needs with which to purify us of our selfishness. Here is quite enough 'trial', 'temptation', 'darkness', 'distress'; there is no need to look for more. But we must allow the Holy Spirit to use it all. This is where we fail to 'take trouble', to make the effort of faith to rise above the level of our senses.

If we have glimpsed the truth of what Jesus is to us by the Father's gift, if we steadfastly believe this truth, then we know that we are indeed in the Promised Land. This is a way of saying that each one of us has been crucified with Christ, has died with Christ and been raised with him. However, we can live as if we were huddled at the edge, not interested in the wonderful life that is offered to us, with little or no desire to explore the land, to nourish ourselves on its riches. This is because, in our heart of hearts, we doubt its reality. We do not really believe that it is a reality for US.

In *The Last Battle,* the final story of C.S. Lewis' *Narnia* tales, the treacherous Dwarfs 'refuse to be taken in,' that is, into the transformed Narnia, even though in reality they have already crossed its threshold. While the children and all the good and noble, whether beast or human, who have fought bravely in the last battle are enraptured by the beauty of all around them, the Dwarfs are insensible to it. For them, this enchanting land is nothing but 'a pitch-black, poky, smelly hole of a stable.'

> 'Are you blind?' said Tirian.
> 'Ain't we all blind in the dark?' said Diggle.
> 'But it isn't dark, you stupid Dwarfs,' said Lucy. 'Can't you see? Look up! Can't you see the sky and the trees and the flowers? Can't you see me?'
> 'How in the name of all Humbug can I see what ain't there?'
> 'Oh the poor things! This is dreadful,' said Lucy. Then she had an idea. She stooped and picked up some wild violets.
> 'Listen, Dwarf,' she said. 'Even if your eyes are wrong, perhaps your nose is all right: can you smell that?' She leaned across and held the fresh, damp flowers to Diggle's ugly nose. But she had to jump back quickly in order to avoid a blow from his hard little fist.
> 'None of that!' he shouted. 'How dare you! What do you mean by shoving a lot of filthy stable-litter in my face?'

Tenderhearted Lucy is desperate to help them to see and feel as she does, but to no avail. She cries through her tears to Aslan as he comes among

76

them: 'could you – will you – do something for
these poor Dwarfs?' 'Dearest,' replies Aslan, 'I will
show you both what I can, and what I cannot do.'
Yet whatever he does for the miserable Dwarfs is
misconstrued and their final word is one of a pitiful
triumph:

> 'Well, at any rate there's no humbug here. We haven't
> let anyone take us in. The Dwarfs are for the Dwarfs.'
> 'You see,' said Aslan, 'they will not let us help them.
> They have chosen cunning instead of belief. Their
> prison is only in their minds, yet they are that prison;
> and they are so afraid of being taken in that they
> cannot be taken out.'
>
> (C.S. Lewis, *The Last Battle*)

We would be exceptional people if we had not
something of a Dwarf mentality lurking within us,
refusing a full commitment to belief, to the utter
reliability of Love. Lewis selects the unexpected
word 'cunning' to juxtapose with 'belief' in a way
that provokes reflection. Deep within every human
heart – unless it has been profoundly purified –
there lurks a sly, unrecognized cunning, all too
well skilled in self-deception and evasion. This is
the total adversary of belief. It is the cunning of
pride, of self-possession, of self-sufficiency. To live
fully out of our inheritance, to live solely by the
faith of the Son of God, to live the life of Jesus –
all this may sound beautiful (and beautiful it indeed
is, beyond our wildest dreams), but in practice it
strikes a deadly blow at human pride. This is why
so many, face to face *in reality* with the self-dispos-
session that life in Jesus calls for, walk no more

with him – not in the sense of complete desertion and denial of belief, but rather because they have said 'No' to *his* Cross, however many other crosses they may be carrying supposedly in his name.

Each of us has the choice either to live by faith or to live by 'flesh'. To live by 'flesh' is to live within the limits of our own potential, within the limits of our own perception and understanding, according to how things seem and feel, according to our natural *experience*. It is instinctive for us to live thus, taking for granted that our conscious experience is to be trusted, that it is the way things really are, the way we are, the way God is – that this *is* our life. We want to remain on this level because it is within our grasp; it is 'ours' and affords a sort of security and assurance. This is so natural to us, even to us religious people, that we are unaware of how much of our life is lived from self, relying on self and not on faith in the Son of Man. We cannot rid ourselves of this deeply rooted pride and self-possession by our own strength. Only the Holy Spirit of the Crucified and Risen One can effect it, and this he is indeed always trying to do. But we must recognize his work, and respond 'Amen'. In the Gospel of John, Jesus speaks of *working* for 'the food that endures for eternal life.' (Jn 6.27). A peasant audience would have known the meaning of labour well. We have to labour to do the 'work of God.' 'This is the work of God, that you believe in him whom He has sent.' (Jn 6.29)

The mystical life, in the theological sense, is not to be identified with specific states of consciousness.

It is rather – as has already been indicated – a matter of the Holy Spirit of Jesus working in our inmost depths, depths inaccessible to ourselves. The Spirit purifies us of all that is not of Jesus, and at the same time constantly increases our capacity for Jesus' divine life. This mystical life is what God wants for us and offers to us at all times, most fully through the sacraments. But there is also another indispensable vehicle for this mystical union: focused, personal prayer.

Prayer is not just our doing; it is a gift. It is not communion with an unidentified divinity – were this the case, everything would depend on our effort, on our getting it right, and the only assurance available that we had done so would be our experience. On the contrary, prayer is communion with the God and Father of Jesus, through Jesus in the Holy Spirit – a communion that is *there,* for us to be taken into. We do not have to discover the secret of gaining entrance; we are already within that encircling love. All we have to do is to affirm it. Our faithful 'attendance' on it, day after day, ensures that we are drawn ever more deeply into it. What we register in our mind and in our emotions is no criterion of failure or success. 'Success' is guaranteed. The weight of it is on God, not on us – on the God of absolute fidelity. God has sworn total self-commitment to us. Our prayer is Amen. Our staying 'there', refusing to be self-important in prayer or anxious about how we are doing, is a wonderful affirmation of the sheer goodness and fidelity of God. Our daily period of prayer may seem fruitless, but it certainly is not. It opens us to divine wisdom – to Christ who is the wisdom and power of God – a wisdom contrary to mere human wisdom no matter how noble, and never understood by it. It is the wisdom of the crucified One – sheer folly, scandalous! – a wisdom that perceives divine love and love's action where natural wisdom would deride or shrink back in disgust. Divine wisdom gently coaxes us to submit to being purified of self, to being comforted in our helplessness and poverty; it persuades us to surrender control, and to abandon ourselves blindly to love. Without such a period of prayer it is hardly possible for our faith in the sacraments to have the depth that will enable us to receive them fruitfully. Nor is it likely that we shall recognize and respond to God's self-gift in the humdrum of our daily life.

Our senses do not necessarily support our life of faith; on the contrary they can shout denial. God longs for us to live by the faith of Jesus. We are blind; such is the fallen human condition. We do not 'see' God, but Jesus does. God has made *him* our wisdom. We choose to live by *his* 'knowing' the Father, his faith – a faith that was expressed in total abandonment to his Father and a trust in Him throughout all life's vicissitudes, and supremely in his acceptance of death by crucifixion. The 'immeasurable greatness of His power' by which God the Father accomplished the exaltation of Jesus is now at work in us who believe (Eph. 1.17–23). We are enabled to live our lives in this certitude all the time, not just sometimes – and not just in some matters, but in all. The Incarnation means that human life is infinitely holy. Every moment is an opportunity for God to love us and for us to respond to His love. How easy it is at times, perhaps for a lot of the time, to sit down in a miserable heap like the Dwarfs in the *Narnia* story, refusing to believe, 'to be taken in'. 'Not violets – stable litter!'; 'not bread – hard stone!'; 'not an egg – stinging scorpion!' So occasion after occasion for receiving God's love slips by, wasted for ever.

Divine love meets us in the real world and nowhere else: in this moment; in *this* circumstance, painful and humiliating though it may be; in *this* person; in the daily unexciting round of seeming trivialities which afford no measure of self-glorification. Divine love meets us here in our flawed, suffering, human condition, and nowhere else. However correct our theology of the Incarnation, its integration into our lives is no easy matter. Malle, the visionary serving woman in Hilda Prescott's book, *The Man on a Donkey*, muses aloud to the imbecile boy, Wat:

> Wat ... have you thought that He has stained Himself, soiled Himself, being not only with men, but Himself a man. What's that, to be man? Look at me ... He was man, is man, the Maker made himself made. God was un-Godded by His own hand. He was God from the beginning, and now never to be clean again. Never again. Alas! ... All's smitten through with Him. Love, frail as smoke, piercing as a needle – near – here. He that's light has come into the clod ... So yon brown cows, and the grass, and us, all things that's flesh, for that He is flesh, are brothers now to God.
>
> (H.F.M. Prescott, *The Man on a Donkey*)

We cannot conceive how God longs for us to be transformed into the image of His Son, only so that we can become who we really are in God's eternal plan. As it is, we have assumed an identity, consciously or unconsciously – an 'I' that is precious to us and must be guarded jealously with all the ploys that natural wisdom devises. It is to this 'I' that we must die if we are to make a reality of Paul's 'I live no longer I; but lives in me *Christ*' (Gal. 2.20); of Paul's wisdom of the cross replacing all human wisdom. We have died with Christ, have been buried with Christ, in principle only; what is true in principle has to become sheer fact. This is essentially a divine work, but it demands from us – as has already been said – a most generous, constant cooperation, an obedient 'yes!' Great trust is needed to remain convinced that this divine work is going on: in the sacraments, in prayer, in our daily life of self-sacrificing love for our brothers and sisters. It operates secretly, but the more effectively for that, in uninteresting greyness just as much as in dramatic 'dark nights'. We can be sure that the 'ordinary' – our own particular life, our temperament and circumstances – is the perfect arena for it. Human wisdom seeks to assess results, to enquire if we are being 'fulfilled' – and, if this is not happening, it manipulates life and other people to ensure that it does happen. Human wisdom assumes that it knows the shape of human fulfilment and how to attain it. It urges us to evade the humiliating, non-satisfying aspects of life; to seek more rewarding ways of prayer; to seek that which makes us feel good and even holy; and to hide from a self-knowledge that strips us of self-complacency and leaves us poor, unholy, unfulfilled.

How important it is to accept the destruction of our spiritual self-image! When it is endangered, we react like scalded cats. We back off; we scramble around for a way of escape; and then we set about doing what we can to reinstate ourselves. What the Spirit of Jesus asks us to do is lovingly, trustingly to accept the disillusionment. What does it matter that we are shabby and soiled when we have Jesus as our holiness? There is only one holiness, and that is Jesus. His holiness is there for us, and so we can be happy not to have a holiness of our own, one we can enjoy – it would be illusory anyway.

The deep work of purification is done unto us. We cannot even see what needs to be done, and any direct attempt to rid ourselves of ourselves would only boost our self-importance. The 'yes' will be costly, but then so has God's 'yes' to us been costly, and only gradually will we perceive how costly. The divine hand must reach right into our entrails and wrest us from ourselves:

O souls who in spiritual matters desire to walk in security and consolation! If you but knew how much it behoves you to suffer in order to reach this security and consolation, and how without suffering you cannot attain to your desire but rather turn back, in no way would you look for comfort either from God or from creatures. You would instead carry the cross and, placed on it, desire to drink the pure gall and vinegar. You would consider it good fortune that, dying to this world and to yourselves, you would live to God in the delights of the spirit, and patiently and faithfully suffering exterior trials, which are small, you would merit that God fix His eyes on you and purge you more profoundly through deeper spiritual trials in order to give you more interior blessings. Those to whom God grants so signal a favour as to tempt them more interiorly must have performed many services for Him, have had admirable patience and constancy for His sake, and in their life and works have been very acceptable to Him.

(St John of the Cross, *Living Flame of Love*, 2.28)

To repeat: 'suffering' and 'mortification' are there in every life; we do not have to manufacture them. 'Dying to the world' does not mean turning our backs on a wholly secular life if such be our calling; what it means is renouncing the merely human wisdom that has its roots in pride in order to live by divine wisdom which is Jesus Christ and him crucified. The more we ponder the New Testament, the more do we stand in awe at the self-sacrificing 'folly' of God's love for us. When God becomes human it is as the sacrificed one, the one who lays down his life in love. 'Whoever has seen me has seen the Father.' (Jn 14.9) Have we not to say that God sacrificed Himself in creating the world, in becoming 'our God?' It is as if self-sacrifice – which, after all, is the law of all genuine love – lies in the depths of the Divine Reality, of the Supreme Being who is Love. To be taken into that Love, to live with the life of God, must perforce mean that sacrifice becomes our way of being too. God loved the world so much that He held nothing back from us, not even His own Son. Amen to this priceless gift of him who is made our wisdom, our justification, our holiness and atonement. Nothing is wanting to us. All is given. Strengthen us, O Given One, to be a glad Amen.

# CHAPTER EIGHT

# Distractions in Prayer

I have been asked to say something about my battle for prayer and, in particular, what distractions I have, how I cope with dryness and other temptations I face in prayer, and how I overcome them.

In spite of the invitation, I do not think my readers would want to be bored to tears by an account of what goes on in my head during prayer! Distractions are my unfailing companions at prayer; but I have learned that prayer doesn't go on in the head, in the brain-box, but in that secret heart that is choosing to pray and to remain in prayer no matter what it feels like or seems like to me. I am totally convinced that our God, the God we see in Jesus, is all-Love, all-Compassion and, what is more, is all-Gift; is always offering God's own Self as our perfect fulfilment. I believe, through Jesus, that we were made for this and that it is divine Love's passion to bring it to perfect fulfilment in us. So when I set myself to pray I am basing myself on this faith and refuse to let it go. I just take it for granted that, because God is the God of Jesus, all-Love, who fulfils every promise, this work of love is going on, purifying and gradually transforming me. What I actually experience on my conscious level is quite unimportant. In fact I experience nothing except my poor, distracted self.

It is a case of blind trust; not a desperate trust, but the sort of brazen, unshakeable trust a child has in good parents. I see nothing of what is going on, of whether the inner garden is beautiful and blooming or not, and have given up all desire to see it because I want God to have it all. You see, that means I can never have any illusion that whatever has happened and is happening in me is my achievement. My part, that little bit that I can do, is simply never to be discouraged, never to give up even for a few minutes, no matter how disgusted with myself I feel, no matter if I have allowed my mind to dwell on what pleased me instead of looking into the Nothing which faith assures me is my All. I go on refusing to take my head off God's breast (I'm thinking of Rembrandt's painting of the Prodigal Son with his head pressed to his father's heart), and I believe that this obstinate, blind trust is what Our Lord wants more than anything else.

So, I admit that there is a temptation to anxiety and discouragement. It could never lead me to give up prayer but I could waste time on it, dwelling on myself rather than throwing myself on God's love. Formerly, it could have prompted me to seek some other way of going about prayer that would ensure that this endlessly clacking mill of mine had plenty to occupy it, but I have come to understand that, for me, it would be a way of hiding from God, hiding my own spiritual inadequacy from myself. Real prayer is utterly truthful. This is what makes it hard. We have to be there before God as we really are, maybe upset, angry, worried, emotionally at sixes and sevens. This is the self I set in God's loving gaze; this is the little creature He loves and has to deal with. In this way, what are usually thought of as temptations are all turned into real prayer.

# CHAPTER NINE

# The Way to Perfection

On the feast of St Francis, 4 October 1582, in the Convent of the Discalced Carmelite nuns at Alba de Tormes, Teresa of Jesus quietly bled to death, serene on the rock of her own lowliness, laying claim to nothing but the mercy and goodness of God. She never lost consciousness but remained in prayer with a crucifix in her hand. Those around her caught a few murmured words: '*Cor mundum ... Cor contritum ... Ne proicias me.*' At around nine o'clock in the evening, she died. (The night of her death coincided with the reform of the Gregorian calendar by which ten days were suppressed and thus 5 October became the 15 October.)

Teresa left a rich heritage to the Church and the world whose value cannot easily be assessed, but two endowments seem particularly relevant today. Thanks to her ability to express herself with originality and power, thanks to her outgoing and generous nature, Teresa has shared herself with rare largesse. Her warm, radiant personality shines on undimmed in all her writings, but especially in her letters. We have, even now, more than 400 of them. It is there we find a totally unselfconscious revelation of what sanctity really is.

Although theoretically we know better, most of us find it difficult to see the true face of holiness. Instinctively we remove it from all that is too natural or 'worldly', as we would say. Of course we accept that a saint is human but, on the whole, we find it impossible to take on the full implications of this. We would not readily acclaim as holy one who was a shrewd businesswoman who took over the management of her brother's financial affairs because she knew more about such things than he did; or a woman who was well aware of her capti-vating charm and never thought of dimming the headlights but allowed them full play, to the delight of all who approached her – more than that, who consciously employed this charm to gain her own ends. Nor do we readily associate with sanctity one who admitted unashamedly to feeling hurt when her love was not returned, annoyed and angry at times. But it is here that we come up against something crucial to holiness that is little appreciated. Teresa's will was identified with that of our Lord and so everything she was, both her many gifts and her weaknesses, were brought into the orbit of her love and dedication. Union with Christ does not mean becoming someone different, renouncing our gifts, changing our temperament, but putting everything we have into our love for God and opening everything we are to his trans-forming influence. Teresa's business acumen, her charm, her wit: everything was caught up into her self-offering to him. And it is above all in her letters that her richly various personality is revealed; there, too, her sanctity.

For this woman, God, revealed to her in Jesus, is the sole Reality. She lived always face to face with Reality. All else – people, events, commonplace things such as medicines, cooking stoves, lawsuits, illnesses, a lizard in a cornfield, a beautiful morning in May when the birds are singing, the cold, rain, floods (cause of so much suffering), the discomfort of the springless wagons in which she journeyed, the bad inns – all the multitudinous events of her life were real to her, had meaning for her only in God. Teresa reached the full potential of personhood; what she was meant to be, she became. This is holiness. Whatever our stature, great or little; whatever our talents, many or few; everything must be given over to God, unified, directed by the desire to make God our all. Teresa was not afraid of humanness. No gift that God, through circum-stances, asked her to develop was left to wither. Develop it she did, unafraid, looking only to him, his approval, not wondering whether she was conforming to an image of holiness or not. That quiet bleeding to death of cancer of the womb has its own poignancy. The medical cause of her death was concealed from her nuns, presumably because it seemed too unworthy of a saint: too natural, earthy, sexual.

This magnificent woman, wholly fulfilled in God, poured all she had, gifts both natural and divine, into the creation of her Carmel, and herein lies another of her outstanding legacies to the world. Teresa's mind was the mind of Christ, his vision hers, and having grasped that the essence of holiness is one with perfect humanity, she was intent on establishing a way of life in which every single feature would aim directly at this holiness. Everything not solely directed towards this end would be pared away. She was writing large, in sharp characters, the very ABC of holiness. She knew in a burning, living way that we are only for God and become ourselves only in surrendering to God. This surrender means, simply, a progressive choice of God's will at every moment, under whatever form it presents itself. And this, in its turn, demands a continuing detachment from all that is not God. All the entanglements of the human heart have to be unwound or severed; the basic inward twist of the human ego has to be reversed so that God's will is recognized and freely embraced.

Teresa grasped what it means to be a solitary. It is a thing of the heart when a man or woman accepts to live nakedly exposed to the living God. This exposure, this emptiness and poverty, is the prerequisite for pure trust in God alone and is what the Gospel is all about. Material solitude in itself cannot effect this nakedness. Teresa saw that it could even provide an escape from it. In her own long struggle to give herself to God she had learned the essential part others play in forging us in holiness. The Rule she was restoring was largely eremitical in structure, though it had progressively acquired some communal elements. Far from lessening these communal aspects, Teresa developed them. She maintained an admirable balance between material solitude and community. There were to be hours of solitary prayer and of retirement in the cell, kept in strict silence. But at the same time she established a carefully controlled community life. Thus the benefits of both were stripped of their dangers. The spirit of Carmel is totally eremitical: to be alone with God alone, which is the human vocation itself. Yet the communal element in Carmel is not a concession to human weakness but the principal means of attaining true solitude. In showing us a particular way, of the greatest clarity, Teresa shows us the whole Way.

Within the little, enclosed world of Carmel there are exactly the same occasions as in the wider world when our wills are crossed, our self-love wounded, what we think of as our rights are disregarded; when we feel put upon, passed over, disliked. There are situations that stir ambition, envy, covetousness. Life can seem colourless and monotonous, prayer difficult, other people hard to live with. The Carmelite way of life fosters a very deep faith that prompts a generous acceptance and response to God in these difficulties and temptations. Possibly because of the intensity of the life and the lack of diversion, their impact is stronger. St Teresa understood that such commonplace happenings, which fill every human life in the cloister or out, are used by God to purify us of our selfishness, if we respond as we should. Through them we learn our helplessness and poverty and, in faith, confidently surrender that poverty to him. Such things as status, qualifications, ascendancy of any kind, must never become securities and escapes. In Carmel, thanks to the wisdom of Teresa, they cannot be.

It is very difficult for us humans to accept our basic condition of poverty and yet it presses upon us from all sides. We cannot control our world; we are at the mercy of others and of what often seems a blind fate. Even our own selves escape us. We are not what we would like to be: inadequacies of all kinds dog us. We are prey to physical and psychological ills. We long to be masters of our lives, in control, strong and beautiful. In a word, gods. The Gospel message is good news to the poor: 'Be human, not God.' This poverty, revolting as it is to our nature, is blessed when it is accepted because it opens us to God and makes us realize our need for a Saviour. Aware that we can never find fulfilment in ourselves, we are drawn to look to him alone. It is to little ones, those who accept to be thus poor, that the secrets of God are revealed. Teresa's Carmel exists to acclaim and acclaim again what it means to be a little one in the Gospel sense.

St Teresa was convinced that her Carmel was apostolic to the core, that it was for others. It is not so much a matter of actually formulating prayers as living the human vocation common to all at such depth of faith that the saving presence of Jesus is made present in the world. For many people God seems sadly absent from the humdrum and everyday. The Carmelite who is living her vocation is, in fact, proclaiming: 'Surely the Lord is in this place and we do not realize it. How awesome our everyday world! Nothing less than the house of God and the gateway to him.' (c.f. Gen. 28.16–17)

Many people carry a romantic notion of Carmel. For those who enter it this is quickly destroyed. Almost always there is the shock, the scandal almost, of ordinariness. In Teresa's thought this blessed ordinariness is where God is, where we meet him and surrender to him. The sole 'specialness' of Carmel is simply to isolate the essential ingredients and live them in an intense, absolute way for the sake of all. It may seem a far cry from Carmelite nun to politician, civil servant, actress, or mother of a growing family. Speaking spiritually, there is no difference. Their lives are made up of the same ingredients; all have the same path to holiness.

# CHAPTER TEN

# Doctor of the Dark Night

It is significant that when Juan de Yepes, known in religious life as Juan de San Matía, threw in his lot with St Teresa of Avila in her work of reform, he changed his name to Juan de la Cruz. What did 'of the Cross' mean to John? He seems to have had a veritable passion for suffering and he seems, too, to have sought it for himself. For him, all that mattered in his life was to respond with his whole being to God's self-bestowal. As with Jesus, no price was too high. Better to enter into life maimed and lame, better to lose the whole world, than to lose that which makes one truly human. 'For the sake of the joy set before him, he endured the cross, despising the shame.' (Hel. c12:2.) The cross, for John, was essentially a sharing in the Cross of Christ.

The Cross is the mysterious design of God for our glorification. We must not identify it with pain as such. Its significance lies, not in the physical and mental torment of him who hung upon it, but in his obedience, his passionate surrender to God; and it is these we must make our own. We have only God's word, Jesus' word, that it is utter blessedness, a real sharing of God's own happiness and fullness of being. Faith, obedience, surrender in trust must be our response. We are called to a fulfilment that surpasses the capacity of our natural powers not merely to attain but even to conceive.

This call to share God's own life defines our existence from birth. Born into natural life with a potential for receiving God himself, the sign of the Cross is upon us. John grasped with extraordinary clarity what is, in fact, central to the Gospel message: that only God can bring us to himself; and he drew out the consequences with ruthless logic.

We are born to die, yet have a tenacious attachment to our natural being, a need for the created world and a will towards happiness, security, fulfilment as we conceive these things. Instinctively we want to live life on our own terms, in our world, not God's. Even when we think we want God, it is as often as not with our own conditions, our own expectations. We have to die to this self-centredness. (St Paul would call it 'flesh' or 'nature'.) Jesus himself tells us that such a radical renunciation is impossible for us. Only God can effect it, and this he wills to do for it is essential to our happiness. John saw clearly that this work of purgation is not wrought by God from a distance: it is the actual effect of God's self-bestowal, an 'inflowing of God into the soul whereby he purges it of its habitual ignorances and imperfections.' (Dark Night Book 2:c.5.) There is a process of substitution: the life of Jesus, God's life, replacing that of the ego.

We cannot go so far as to say that this summons to creatures of earth to transcend their natural limitations explains all suffering, but we do know that suffering of any kind can become, in God's providence, a powerful means of purification. This explains something of John's passion for it:

> If you did but know how necessary it is to suffer and endure in order to reach this security and consolation … you would in no way seek consolation, either from God or from creatures, but would rather bear the Cross and, having embraced it, would desire to drink pure gall and vinegar.
>
> (St John of the Cross, *Living Flame of Love*, st. II)

'Security,' 'consolation' – are not these what we are always seeking, implicitly or explicitly? They are to be found in God alone. Suffering shakes our supposed security, reveals our helplessness, brings home to us, often with cruel force, that we cannot control life. It brings us, time and time again, up against the mystery of life, its unfairness, its topsy-turviness. Superficial images of God are swept away. God does not conform. He is baffling, inscrutable in his ways and, as far as our experience of life is concerned, there is little to commend him. With Jesus we must believe, utterly, that this unfathomable Mystery is Love and must live our lives in this faith.

The 'inflowing of God into the soul' that purges and transforms is what John means by mystical contemplation. 'contemplation', because it comprises a mysterious, obscure knowledge of God infused into the human spirit, a knowledge that cannot be grasped hold of but that inevitably sets the inmost

heart on fire with love and desire, often very secretly.
This mystical contemplation is not the reserve of a
small elite; it is nothing else than God himself,
communicating himself directly in love, and it is for
all. Sadly, though, we block him; we do not want
God; we want ourselves and a God who fits our
own requirements. Moreover we are not prepared to
do what we can to clear the way for him:

> It behoves us to note the reason why there are so few
> that attain to this lofty state of the perfection of union
> with God. It must be known that it is not because God
> is pleased that there should be so few ... for it would
> rather please him that all souls should be perfect. But
> it is rather that he finds few vessels who can bear so
> high and lofty a work ... They are not strong and
> faithful in little things.
> (St John of the Cross, *Living Flame of Love*, st. II)

John takes a fine toothcomb and rakes through the
whole of our human experience. The effect is
similar to what happens to our assumption that we
observe the commandments when we read the
Sermon on the Mount: complacency is shattered
and we beat our breast along with the publican. We
see that much of our life is lived merely instinctively, selfishly, whereas,

> every satisfaction offered to the sense that is not for the
> honour and glory of God must be renounced and
> rejected for the love of Jesus Christ who, in this life,
> had and sought no other pleasure than doing the will
> of the Father.
> (St John of the Cross, *Ascent of Mount Carmel*,
> I.xiii)

Let us note that there is no instance in the Gospel where Jesus taught us to inflict pain on ourselves for religious purposes. He set us free from such manipulative practices. The early Church quickly fell into some of them, as though the sheer weight of the Good News were unbearable without their support. Jesus relieves us of the doubt and anxiety that compels us to do these things, giving us the glorious certainty of God's absolutely *unconditional* love. To accept this with all our heart and stake everything on it is the self-denial of the Gospel. How hard! But we are exposed to Divine Compassion, not to the hard gaze of a task-master, and can thus accept without anxiety to be answerable for every deliberate thought, word and deed. Grounding ourselves in God's love alone, renouncing every other security, whether from within or without, we are content to live without certainties, even with confusion. Today, we have our own peculiar 'night' in that what we had assumed to be religious certainties, perhaps even basic principles, have collapsed. In the West, the Church we have loved and in which we have invested ourselves, is rapidly losing credibility and we may well be wondering what *is* certain, what is reliable.

John would sympathize with this, but bid us recognize the wonderful opportunity we now have for profound faith and trust in the one certainty we have: the God of Jesus and his fidelity. The danger is, of course, that instead of allowing ourselves to be engulfed in Mystery, in the God who is ever greater, we dither and avoid commitment. Part of our commitment is to recognize our need of, and responsibility towards, the community of believers we call the Church, our need for the supports of religion, and especially the sacraments. Commitment to the God who has come to us in lowly humanity induces us to bear with humility – though never abdicating our personal responsibility – the yoke of the institution, even when it nearly breaks the heart and strains credulity and loyalty to the limit.

Each of us has a unique vocation, humanly speaking, forged of inheritance, personal history, temperament, talents and our present context. We are called in our individuality, with its possibilities, but also with its limitations, to perfect discipleship, to love of one another 'as I have loved you.' No one can tell another how to do this. Each of us must rely on the Lord, desire with all desire to please him, and then act. We are not asked never to make a mistake, never to put a foot wrong. Neither Jesus nor John of the Cross counsel acts of self-denial as though these had value in themselves. Each must have an actual purpose. Jesus deliberately dissociated himself from the Baptist's ascetic image. How readily could the judgement be made: here, in the Baptist, is the man of God! But there, one of ourselves – fond of his food and drink! Whatever else their significance, the meals Jesus took in company reveal his simple acceptance of the smiling side of life. He knows that the Father carries out his work of purification and transformation of human hearts in ordinary life: where men and women work and play, love and marry, eat and sleep, there the Kingdom of God is among you. Would not most of us prefer definite direction, rules of conduct, ascetic practices, even quite tough ones if, having accomplished them, we could feel safe and relax? But God does not want this. He wants us to trust him enough to live with him unafraid, totally defenceless in his presence. We can truly say that John of the Cross' teaching has as its sole aim to bring us to this inner poverty, which is our truth:

> And when we shall have been brought to nothing, when our humility is perfect, then will take place the union of the soul and God, which is the highest and noblest estate attainable in this life.
>
> (c.f. St John of the Cross, *Ascent of Mount Carmel*, II.vii).

# CHAPTER ELEVEN

# St Thérèse of Lisieux and the Holy Child

Were it not for Jesus, the Mystery in which we are inescapably enfolded would remain for us an impenetrable darkness and our hearts an endless yearning. As it is, in him we see that the Mystery is absolute love, totally *unconditional* – how important that word, and how difficult for us to 'realize'! – and that this love, unconditional though it is and something that will never be withdrawn, calls for an appropriate response. Jesus knew, as no other ever could, the immensity of love for humankind issuing from the God whom he called 'Father'. His whole life and surrender in death was his passionate 'yes' to this love – a love too great for his human heart to hold without breaking.

Thérèse of Lisieux entered deeply into the mystery of Jesus and lived out her short life surrendered to him, and was forever pondering on his words and deeds. However, there were two 'moments' in Jesus' life that unveiled to her the inmost nature of love and that inspired and shaped her response: his infancy and his Passion. In both, the Son of God is defenceless, vulnerable, delivered up to human hands. Here was something that caught at her heart and on which she dwelt incessantly. Love can only be love and nothing else. It must offer itself nakedly and be received in its nakedness. Thérèse understood that the divine omnipotence is the omnipotence of love and only that. To be true to itself it must come to us with no false trappings of power but as what it is, pure self-gift that humbles itself, divests itself of 'god-ness' (that is, of all the qualities that *we* attach to divinity) and 'stoops to nothingness to transform that nothingness into love.'

It seems that for *little* Thérèse – and it was as such that she always saw herself – in her *little,* ordinary life, it was more important to relate to omnipotent Love in the *little* Jesus. The divine Infant was as dependant for his life on the loving protection and care of Mary and Joseph as is any human child on its parents. What did this not say about the immensity and *tenderness* of divine Love! We find Thérèse expressing, over and over again, the quality of tenderness. God's heart is more tender than that of the most tender of mothers. She herself had experienced from her family an unfailing tenderness that had nurtured, guided, protected and upheld her. How could such a tenderness not abound in and flow from God's own heart? She recognized that tenderness stoops to frailty even to experiencing it along with us. And she would have us purge our hearts of any notion of a distant, aloof and severe deity, an idol that can lie – in both meanings of the word! – within the human psyche, no matter how well-informed the mind. Tenderness is a reverent, almost worshipful response to what is weak, small, vulnerable, dependant. It longs to cherish and protect the fragile preciousness and beauty of being. What human person is not flawed and fragile? True love discerns this and responds with tenderness. Such is God's love for each one of us. He is 'wrapped up in', intent on each one and filled with reverent tenderness towards us.

Divine love approaches us where we are and as we are, like to us in all things save sin. Christians of the first era would hymn the 'self-emptying' of Jesus in his solidarity with us and in his obedience unto death. Thérèse saw and hymned it in the Child. We can see her portrayed in a photograph holding a double picture: on the one side of Veronica's veil with its imprint of Jesus' bruised and bleeding face; on the other a rather magisterial looking boy. This image of the divine Child is not what Thérèse had in mind. She was thinking of an infant, a toddler, one who needs looking after, who needs toys to play with – she offered herself as a 'toy' for his delight; one who, being irrational, is capricious, playing with a toy, sticking pins in his ball, tiring of it, throwing it aside and forgetting all about it. All this sounds childish, if not ridiculous. Which of us would find devotion in thinking of our relationship to God like that? Yet behind these childish images lies the reality of an incomparably selfless love. There was nothing childish in the wise young adult Carmelite, wholly detached from herself, devoted entirely to God and to others. Thérèse never lived an adult life in the outside world, and Carmel at that time did not offer a wide range of the reading that would have expanded her imagination and emotions. Inevitably, her images tend to be drawn from childhood – and an exceedingly sheltered childhood at that. Yet for all her profuse use of the French words *petit/petite* there was no trace of pettiness in this splendid girl.

On the occasion of her Clothing in the habit of the Order, Thérèse extended her name. She became Sr Thérèse of the Infant Jesus *and of the Holy Face*, that is, of the suffering, humiliated Face of Jesus, devoid of human beauty, despised and shunned as lepers were despised and shunned. Here was God, infinite Beauty, Goodness and Love, *hidden, unrecognized, despised*! It is impossible to fully understand Thérèse's devotion to Jesus' infancy without the backdrop of her contemplation of the Holy Face, and therefore something must be said about it.

There is no doubt that her adored father's humiliating mental derangement, which began shortly after her entrance into Carmel, gave poignant significance to what was already a devotion in the community. Seemingly aware at times of his condition, M. Martin would throw a veil over his face as if to hide his shame. The mystery of this despised, divine Face took more and more hold on Thérèse as she experienced life in the monastery, grew in self-knowledge and suffered. Jesus' Passion dominates the letters she wrote to support her sister Céline who was nursing the invalid. In caressing his stricken face and wiping his tears, Céline, she says, is tenderly succouring the face of Jesus. A stigma attached to mental illness, and the daughters were aware of the mutterings about 'religious mania' and the hurtful insinuations that it was the loss of his youngest daughter that had tipped the aged father into madness. The young Carmelite witnessed the once distinguished face of her 'King' now 'hidden' and 'despised': an icon of Jesus.

For Thérèse, the mysteries of the infancy and the Man of Sorrows both expressed the same divine truths: the inexpressible nature of God's tender, compassionate love for us, a love that will stop at nothing but will pour out its all to us and for us and, at the same time, the humble longing of this love for a return of its love. God chooses to be *needy*. And what more needy than a child? Therefore this is what he became. So Thérèse learned more and more that our response is necessary if this need of divine love to be loved is to be satisfied. We, and we alone, can free the immensity of divine love to do its will, do justice to itself: to take hold of our littleness and bring each one of us to blissful fulfilment in his love. This alone can satisfy his heart – and ours. Divine love has made itself powerless as it crosses the frontier 'in human form', leaving 'divinity' on the other side and with it, all that that might mean in terms of power and self-protection. From now on, divine love in person is in our hands to do as we please with it. Yes, in a real sense, God is powerless in the world. He saves only *through* 'man', through

Jesus. And the risen Jesus continues his saving mission through the Church, that is, through the faith and love of believers – of ourselves. God positively *needs* us; he is powerless without us. It is not our works of themselves that he needs, but our love. And for this he thirsts. Thérèse would say that we who know and love him must forget ourselves and devote our entire lives to satisfying this divine thirst: we must bring him 'souls'.

Thérèse greeted the divine helplessness and longing with passionate tenderness; she embraced this 'little one', her God, in utter abasement and enfolded him in protective love. One finds in her an awe-inspiring selflessness of love. It is Jesus alone who matters, never Thérèse! This process began at her so-called 'conversion' which, significantly, took place in her fifteenth year on a Christmas night. Thus it was the newborn Lord, become little and weak for her, who lifted her out of her neurotic self-preoccupation and gave her strength. In vain she had tried to overcome her own weakness; suddenly, on this blessed night, it happened. She found herself seemingly miraculously changed. Though rich, he had become poor so that we might be rich, and weak so that we might be clothed with his strength. Thérèse experienced this truth and it influenced her for the rest of her life. Her human 'can't' was transformed by Jesus into a 'can'. What is impossible to human beings is possible to God. From that moment her real spiritual life began. She was given light to understand and feel to her depths how little Jesus was known and loved, and she resolved to spend her life catching his precious, redeeming blood and applying it to 'souls'. She herself began to thirst with him. No longer was she interested in her own, personal spiritual life – that she could safely leave to God – but her whole intent was to love Jesus. She realized that it is the love of his lovers that in a mysterious, hidden way 'brings souls to him'.

When we reflect earnestly, is it not true that, to a large extent, we implicitly assume that it is for God to wipe the tears away from us, to put things right for us, to console us? Behind this is there not an image of an 'Almighty God' who, if he really wanted to, could make things a lot easier? Why doesn't he, if he is love? We get petulant and, secretly at least, feel let down, badly treated. Isn't all the giving on our side! Why doesn't he change our inner state, give us consolation and show us that he loves us? Thérèse completely reversed this all-too-human selfishness and what she did we also can do. Our faith sings joyously at Christmas: 'Oh come ye to Bethlehem!' and, as we see in a newborn babe the 'God from God, Light from Light', we adore him. This faith, and faith alone, reveals and shows us God in what seems to be not-God. In Jesus we have the full, definitive revelation of the divine splendour in profound hiddenness. Mysteriously, where it seems most hidden, there it is most truly manifest. This revelation continues. God comes to us in the human, in our own humanity and in the ordinariness of our everyday lives. This is where he is for us, and nowhere else. There is no 'mystical' realm into which, if we try hard enough we have a right to be transported and where we shall feel wonderful and no longer the rather drab little people we are. Thérèse saw what we miss – maybe we choose not to see it – the preciousness of the ordinary. Far from wanting something more 'divine', she positively loved the ordinary; a sanctity, hidden from itself, the sanctity *of little ones*. This, she says, 'is the *truest* and the *most holy*, and it is the type I desire.' She contemplated Jesus' hidden life at Nazareth, and the holiness of his mother, simple, hidden, unselfconscious. We can be praying to a god who does not exist, 'out there', detached, who can look after us, protect us, shower us with blessings of a kind we understand. But the only God is the God of Jesus, who gives nothing less than God's own Self, and who alone can fully satisfy the human heart. Here lies the reason for God's hiddenness, for the darkness and aridity that we find so baffling and disquieting. The true God can reveal his true self *only* in the human, and this means in the very warp and weft of our unique humanness and day-to-day lives. The treasure of divine love is all around us here and now, whoever, wherever we are. Everything is an opportunity for receiving and responding to God's love.

Thérèse saw this naked, unadorned, vulnerable love entrusting itself to us, and yet meeting with lack of comprehension, if not contempt. Where we cry: 'This can't be God' because we don't want God to be like that, she holds out the arms of her love to what her faith reveals as the very excess and folly of divine love. This is the meaning of her devotion to Jesus' childhood, to the mystery of his chosen neediness. Never must she 'hurt' him by lack of understanding, by making a fuss of aridity, of life's little difficulties. The Infant needs his sleep, don't be selfish and try to wake him up to smile at you! It is for you to caress him and dry his tears, not for you to make demands on him with your fretting, your anxieties about yourself! Thérèse completely reversed the natural human attitude. She encouraged sisters who sought her advice to caress the divine infant, bring him gifts of flowers, smile upon him and sing to him. These are her images for a practical living out of love, doing everything for love and not for self, forgetting oneself in order to make others happy, denying self-will, bearing patiently with sufferings of mind and body. It is this selfless love that mysteriously enables God's love to effect an entrance into hearts that are closed. 'The Almighty has given (us) *as fulcrum*: HIMSELF ALONE; as *lever*: PRAYER which burns with a fire of love.' This is the omnipotent force that 'lifts the world'. Recollection of the awesome mystery of Jesus' passion does not dominate Thérèse's daily life; rather, she keeps a light, childlike, gracious tone, playful and witty. Thérèse never dramatized her difficulties – they were pinpricks and only that – the Child playing with his toy!

Thérèse saw the preciousness of ordinariness, and this insight was given to her for our sake. She lived ordinariness to the full. We must take very seriously what she tells us of her own weakness, littleness and imperfections. She really is one of us, having to bear the burden of her own unique

human-ness. Her God's unutterable tenderness in
choosing to become a human being, experiencing
for himself 'how frail you have made the children
of men!' enabled her confidently to acknowledge
and live in the truth of her being not-God, unspiritual, 'of the earth earthy', quite incapable in
herself of reaching God. This is our truth too,
reluctant as our pride is to accept it. In what is our
natural habitat we may be self-assured and capable,
but once we seriously desire to give God first place
in our lives, we begin to experience ourselves differently. We are not competent at all. We feel
ourselves inadequate. The whole revelation of God
in Jesus gives us the absolute certainty that God has
come down to us to lift us up, to do for us what we
cannot do for ourselves. Of course, what we can do
we must do. Thérèse takes this for granted and her
generosity knew no bounds. We must look for
God's will at every hour and surrender to it
whatever the cost. But try as we may, we shall fall
short. Thérèse begs us to understand that all God
really wants is our blind trust that he will do everything for us. Like a toddler, all we can do, spiritually speaking, is lift our little foot to the first
step of the stairs and go on trying. Jesus, like a
mother, will come down and carry us up in his
arms. 'Ah Jesus! Why can't I tell all *little souls*
how unspeakable is Your condescension? I feel
that if You found a soul weaker and even more
little than mine (which is impossible) You would be
pleased to grant it still greater favours, provided it
abandoned itself with total confidence to Your
Infinite Mercy.'

116

Thérèse lived her truth to the end. Eighteen months before her death from tuberculosis there suddenly fell upon her a hitherto unimaginable suffering: the complete obscuration of her faith. For the first time she confronted in herself the possibility of stark unbelief, the reality of atheism: no heaven, no God – nothing; everything that gave meaning and joy to her life, gone. Unless upheld by him on whom she had always relied to transform her human 'can't' into a 'can', she would despair, she would sin. Affirming her belief in his reality she maintained a steadfast peace and abandonment in the horrible darkness that echoed with mocking, blasphemous voices. The orientation of her whole being was focused on Jesus and away from herself. Jesus matters, not Thérèse. Suffering within and without to an unbearable degree, experiencing a despoliation that seemed not only physical but spiritual too, Thérèse's childlike, charming 'lightness' disguised the full extent of her anguish. Knowing her Beloved grieved over her sufferings she would have liked to conceal them even from him! Shortly before her death, she composed a song, *Une rose éfeuillée*. Its typically gracious imagery cannot conceal the passion of her self-squandering love as she confronts her dissolution.

A rose that has just reached its perfection, she deliberately, lovingly, tenderly sheds her petals under the feet of the divine Child, her 'Treasure, Beauty Supreme', as he takes his first steps on 'our sad earth', and as he treads his last to Calvary. That is the meaning of her life – to be all for Jesus, for his easing, for his joy. This is not merely Thérèse *loving*. Thérèse is possessed by Love and has herself become love.

# CHAPTER TWELVE

# Thoughts on the Doctorate of St Thérèse

In St Thérèse we celebrate something of a phenomenon. She died before reaching her twenty-fifth birthday; never left her Carmelite enclosure once she had entered it nine years earlier; was canonized with what was then unprecedented speed; hailed by Pius XI as the greatest saint of modern times and, in fact, has any saint been more popular? What is more, she is a Doctor of the Church, alongside the array of solemn greybeards: Athanasius, Cyril, Augustine, Bernard, to name but a few. This was an all male assembly until, in 1970, St Teresa of Avila, our Foundress, and the Dominican tertiary, St Catherine of Siena, invaded the male stronghold – rather exotic female saints, one has to admit! And, since 1997, our little Thérèse ... To get an idea of her background, what one might call its intellectual and cultural poverty, we have only to take a look at some of the published literature about her. Unless we know something about where she was coming from –

what nourishment she had, the culture, the atmosphere, the historical space in which she loved God with such passion and surrendered herself to His loving purpose – we can't get hold of the meaning of Thérèse herself.

What is the meaning of it all? Why is this young woman so very important in the life of the Church? Why is she considered a Doctor of the Church, a teacher of the true faith, the faith of Jesus? She wrote a simple autobiography. Originally it was intended to give pleasure to, and written at the request of, one of her older sisters who had been elected Prioress. The Prioress who succeeded her asked Thérèse to finish it. This is followed by another section containing the greater part of two letters she wrote to her oldest sister. The style, typical of her class and times, has deceived many, depriving them of the treasures this artless book contains. The same goes for her many letters to members of her community and to her family, together with the very few she wrote beyond that circle.

Thérèse broke new ground, cutting through firmly established and firmly held positions in regard to the spiritual life. One might say with truth that she abolished the 'spiritual life' understood as it was (and, alas, still is), as a sort of specialized area of human life, particularly Christian life: a sort of spiritual culture that functioned according to its own rules, bore clearly defined features and had its own divisions and subdivisions. Instead, Thérèse returned us to the Gospel with its wonderful but daunting simplicity, focusing our eyes on Jesus alone and on the *Abba*, the Father, he shows us, and turning them away from all interest in ourselves and our 'spiritual lives'. Now this is marvellous, good news to humble folk; but it can be off-putting and annoying to those who are really using God to boost their own image of themselves. Thérèse is very, very challenging when understood correctly. Her sheer simplicity can dismay.

Towards the end of her life it seems Thérèse had certainty that her way, her 'little way', as she called it, was meant for others: for a vast, innumerable army of little souls, ordinary people. She yearned that all the ordinary, little folk who follow Jesus should grasp for themselves that absolute holiness was for them, that each one of them was called to the closest possible union with God. People just didn't believe that. Do you, really? They took it for granted that they would be lucky just to scrape in and that sainthood was for the privileged, gifted few – well, like the great Saints, Teresa and Catherine of Siena, who abounded in visions and ecstasies and so forth. Thérèse, too, thought along these lines to begin with, and she wanted to be big like that, heroic like Joan of Arc whom she admired so much. And then she found it just didn't work for her. She experienced herself always (and we must believe her in this) as, well, as we experience ourselves! Full of human emotions, emotions that don't feel holy and perhaps feel the opposite: wandering thoughts when we should be praying; no sense of God being present; no lovely feelings of fervour ... oh, how far from our preconceptions of what a 'spiritual' person should be and feel like!

Now, I suspect that most of us, deep down, feel that people like us could never come to an immense love of God, that we are not one of the chosen, the favourites. And it may be that deep down we make a decision, perhaps hardly averted to, of therefore not trying very hard, not going all out for it. That is where our Thérèse steps in with passion. We are looking at ourselves; she looked at Jesus, at what he says about the Father's love for us: the lost, the weak, the sick, the sinners – human beings in all their pathetic inadequacy. She leaped out of these natural, discouraging perceptions and reflections and threw her whole weight onto God. She trusted God with a blind, unwavering, daring trust and came to understand that this won the divine Heart as nothing else could. She took the good God 'by the heart', as she said. Far from being discouraged by all that she experienced of herself, she began to see that what she called her poverty, her littleness, her nothingness, was in fact her treasure, provided she opened it all out in boundless trust to God. We should never forget that Thérèse's experience of herself was the same as our own. Thérèse, of course, experienced herself as Thérèse and we experience ourselves as ourselves, but I must stress that she is not speaking of something unknown to any one of us. We can wriggle away from her profound challenge by thinking that, for all she says, she wasn't like us. Her heart burned with love; she had intense, felt desires; she was a saint and we are not. How that would upset her! One of her own sisters, reading something she had written about her desire for martyrdom and her immense desires to love God and do good on earth, gave voice to similar objections ending with: 'I'll never believe that I can love God as you do.' Thérèse pitched in, frustrated and distressed. She went on to explain that, when she had written the particular pages referred to, yes, she had felt those desires but that she put no weight on them. They might disappear and it wouldn't matter, but she would come to harm if she put any confidence in them. She went on to plead: 'Oh, do believe me!' The only thing God loved in her, she said, was to see her love her poverty and the blind trust she had in His mercy. 'These are my sole riches,' she claimed, 'and how can they not be yours too?' She issues the same challenge to each one of us. She gives us no escape route. What she did each of us can also do. Everything she did was what 'ordinary souls' must be able to accomplish. There must be nothing extraordinary in her way. That is her importance in the Church; that is why she is hailed as a great teacher of the faith – perhaps the greatest, who knows?

Nothing extraordinary. And yet Thérèse is extraordinary in her utter generosity. She meant it when she said that she wanted to love God totally. Do we really mean it when we think or say it? I doubt if there would be many in religious life if there were not something of this desire in our hearts; but in Thérèse this desire was transformed into practical action. She made up her mind not to refuse the slightest sacrifice God might ask of her and so, of course, she was on the look out for opportunities for self-giving, for putting others first, for closing her lips, and even her heart, against a complaint or grumble or criticism of another. Her whole intent was to please the good God who loved her so tenderly. She did not always feel this love and, towards the end of her life, a dreadful darkness engulfed her. Then she believed against all feeling, and hoped against hope. Her life, as ours, was filled with little nothings: joys, sorrows, irritations, disappointments, happy surprises, work to be done, sometimes pleasant, sometimes irksome. Tragedy struck for Thérèse – as sooner or later it must do for all of us in one form or another – in the person she loved most on earth, her father, who was afflicted for years by a humiliating mental illness. The last two years of her own short life were marked by severe suffering of mind and body. Thérèse wasted nothing of it, but turned everything into love and she urges us to do the same. Like Jesus she lived her human life in its particularity as Jesus lived his, certain of the Father's love. And this faith bore her through it all, as it bore him through his dreadful Passion.

Each of us is born at a particular moment of history; we have our own background, inheritance, and education: all the things that go to make up one unique, human life. We are all highly conditioned. I have mentioned in passing the cultural and intellectual paucity of Thérèse's background, both at home and in the monastery. Seen from our point of view she had immense disadvantages. Think of this: she never had access to the Bible as a whole, certainly not the Old Testament. All she had was a book of carefully selected extracts. Yet how she used those texts, finding lights in them, interpreting them, often, indeed, out of context, yet to her spiritual profit. She had access to the New Testament, and fed on it, but lacked our access to a wealth of scriptural scholarship. Look at the sentimental, even maudlin holy pictures and artwork she used and no doubt loved! Look at her own sugary-sweet paintings. The whole atmosphere seems stuffy to us and redolent of antimacassars and old lace. That was her culture; that was part of the condition in which she lived and, in that sense, it was inescapable. But, as I have said, she used everything. And her faithful God used everything of it, too, to give her Himself. This is of supreme importance for each of us. None of us can ever excuse ourselves by saying we are handicapped, or that we suffer from this or that disadvantage or we have this or that obstacle to real holiness in our lives. Rather, we must see that each one of us has in his or her life everything necessary for real sainthood: the wherewithal, the environment with which, and in which, to love God with our whole being. It is a case of total trust in our loving Father who only longs to sanctify us and make us totally happy. At the same time, it is for us to make use of everything, every single occasion, even – we might say especially – those that seem to be the most formidable obstacles. Pope John Paul II declared that Thérèse has restored a vibrant sense of our adoption as children to the whole people of God. We need not shrink from this word: 'of God.' She lived as a loved child lives in perfect confidence in its *Abba*, its Father. There is no reason whatever why each of us cannot do the same, if only we use everything that is given to us and trust our poverty to this loving *Abba* of ours. Thérèse lived out to the full the immense, daring confidence that, she believed, was the only possible way for us to come to a great love of God. This can only be received as pure gift, received into an empty heart.

CHAPTER THIRTEEN

# St Elisabeth of the Trinity

Carmelite of Dijon, France, *1880–1906;*
*canonized 1998.*

'There is a Being who is Love who wishes us to live in communion with Him. Oh Mama, it is delightful, for He is there keeping me company, helping me to suffer, urging me to go beyond my suffering to rest in Him; do as I do, you will see how that transforms everything.' Thus Elisabeth Catez, in religion Elisabeth of the Trinity, wrote to her beloved mother two weeks before she died.

Do we have here just one more of Carmel's *wünderkindern*, as a young Sister of my acquaintance dubs the youthful spiritual prodigies with which the annals of Carmel abound? The pattern of their journeys to 'sainthood' is amazingly uniform. Born and brought up in devout families, they have become aware of a religious vocation in childhood; as teenagers they secretly vow their virginity to God; they enter the monastery as soon as possible and edify all by their perfection, their spirit of prayer and words of wisdom liberally dispensed. Longing to express their love for God in suffering, these devout young women offer themselves as 'victims for souls' and then contract a mortal sickness and get the suffering they desire, not infrequently becoming convinced of a special mission to the world in the process. Their excruciating illness is endured heroically; they die, and, behold a saint!

Let us be cautious. In her searching study of St Thérèse of Lisieux, *The Hidden Face*, Ida Görres has uncovered the powerful drive in religious circles towards 'saintliness' of a certain type. Within these circles, a child could fall willing victim to such expectations, for what could be more entrancing to a devout little girl than the beauty, the romance of being a saint, of being one of God's special beloved! The enormous, aspiring psychic energies of youth are poured out in the endeavour, and hardship, even suffering, are readily shouldered. Think what an aspiring ballet dancer will endure to become a *prima ballerina!* It is not easy to distinguish a passionate desire for the image of 'saintliness', a feeling that one is specially favoured and close to God, from a single-minded gift of self to God. Görres points out how everything in Thérèse Martin's *milieu*, the spiritual influences of her childhood and early adolescence, conspired to lead her down this false path; and yet, at a given moment, marvellously enlightened, she turned her back on it and consistently resisted it to the very end of her life. Thérèse perceived how the pursuit of a saintly image could be the driving force motivating religious persons, and she begged God to keep her from illusion and enable her to stand always in the truth, seeing things, including herself, as they really are. Incorruptible, she remained utterly authentic, poor in spirit, humble of heart.

What of Elisabeth? Many features of her short life fit the pattern of the *'wünderkind'* thus described. However, a critical, even sceptical study of her writings and of authenticated facts in her life yields the conviction that here is the real thing, here is sanctity. She lacks, it is true, Thérèse's charm, her humour and playfulness. Moreover, her 258 extant letters from Carmel are 'much of a muchness': read a dozen and you have read the lot. Their tone is uniformly 'elevated' and, when read one after another, they are, frankly, boring. The only difference in their content is a sensitive, compassionate allusion to her correspondent's particular anxiety or need. Yet what a warm, caring heart they reveal! Elisabeth is solemn and takes herself very seriously, but none could doubt the passionate conviction behind every word.

The phenomenon of the genuine young saint always forces us to examine our ideas of holiness. Do we not instinctively tend to see it as bound up with merit and reward? Our natural reaction is that of the Labourers in the Vineyard: 'These have worked but one hour; … we have borne the burden of the day and the heat.' And we go on to compare one saint with another: such a hard life this one had, such suffering, whereas that one had it easy, and so on. But holiness has nothing to do with merit in that sense, with length of service or degrees of suffering in themselves. It can never be a human achievement. Holiness is simply the gift of God's self in love, received and surrendered to in love. Elisabeth let God love her.

Elisabeth of the Trinity was the eldest daughter of Joseph Catez and Marie Rolland. Joseph, son of a poor agricultural labourer, made a successful career for himself in the army, was raised to the rank of Captain and eventually named Chevalier of the Legion of Honour. At the age of thirty-seven he married Marie Rolland, who came from a military family. She was thirty-three. Her first fiancé had been killed in the war of 1870 and for a time Marie had thought of becoming a Religious. Elisabeth was born in a military camp; her sister Marguerite, 'Guite', followed a few years later. Marie was not, especially for those days, a young mother. As her soldier husband was often away, the early education and care of the children devolved almost exclusively on her. Moreover, Joseph died when Elisabeth was seven, and it is not hard to imagine how closely the 'trio,' as they called themselves, clung to one another and became everything for one another. Elisabeth had all the characteristics of the spiritually precocious child and this spiritual precocity enabled her to overcome her ferocious temper. On her sister's testimony she was 'a little devil', falling into furious rages when thwarted. All the same, at seven years old she confided to an elderly priest friend her determination to become a Religious.

As Madame Catez loved travelling, the trio enjoyed delightful holidays in the mountains and by the sea. Elisabeth responded rapturously to nature's beauty and began to 'feel' a divine presence pervading all. It became natural for her to commune with this divine presence in the woods and meadows, in the mountains and by the sea. God was everywhere but most especially within her own heart. 'Let me remain,' she prayed, 'in that hidden recess of my being where I see and feel You so clearly.' What may at first have been a merely natural mysticism was taken up without any rupture into a living faith in the God of Revelation, the God of Jesus. His name was Jesus, and in Jesus she traced the lineaments of the divine Reality and knew Him as Love that gives Himself. The Eucharist, for her, was the sacrament of this divine self-giving. The whole mystery of God and God's out-poured love for us was to be found in it. It would seem that, at an early age, Elisabeth also received what we might call the gift of ecstatic prayer, a sort of experiential knowledge of God's love and presence. Such a gift is not holiness but a means to lead a person to holiness and make his or her life fruitful for others. God has given to each of us, without exception, gifts intended for the same purpose. What matters is that, like Elisabeth, we use them to the full – and how marvellously faithful to them she was! Hers was the temperament of a musician. (In fact, she was a gifted pianist and her general education was neglected in favour of this, since her mother envisaged a musical career for her eldest daughter.) Vibrant to every form of beauty in the natural world, she responded with the same sensitivity and passion to the vision of God's love for His creatures.

Elisabeth held firmly to her childhood's decision and, at seventeen, revealed to Mme Catez her desire to enter Carmel. Stricken to the heart, the mother begged her to wait until she was twenty-one, hoping that, in the meantime, a suitable husband would appear to deflect her from her purpose. Elisabeth yielded to her mother's wish. The cost of this renunciation was confided only to her diary. As far as appearances went, Elisabeth Catez was an attractive young woman of the world, always beautifully groomed and dressed, enjoying long holidays with her friends in their country *châteaux*, joining wholeheartedly, so it seemed, in tennis parties, dancing and walks in the mountains. In trying to assess her response to God's love, her surrender to 'the least wish of the Beloved', these three or four years of waiting, of enduring what was for her an 'exile', with such hidden generosity, must be given their full weight. Spiritually gifted, she developed the graces given and learned the secret of remaining always in the 'cell' of her heart, attentive to the Beloved, even when dancing. Her absorption did not pass unnoticed, least of all by the young men! 'She is not for us. Look at that expression,' one was heard to say to another.

At twenty-one, Elisabeth obtained her heart's desire and entered Carmel. When someone remarked how hard it must be for her to give up music, she retorted immediately that the only sacrifice lay in leaving her mother and sister. The strain of the waiting period, the awareness of the pain she was inflicting on those so dear to her, affected her health. However, once in Carmel she knew she had 'come home' and nothing could dim her intense happiness. Now she was free 'to live alone with the One', as St Teresa of Avila described the vocation of the Carmelite. By nature and by grace Elisabeth was extraordinarily fitted for this vocation and her circumstances were happy in every way: the community was well balanced and fervent; the Prioress, though inexperienced and young, was gentle, kind and with high ideals for her community. Elisabeth loved her. As she was the only novice, the Prioress undertook her formation and a very close relationship developed. Elisabeth died before the formal period of formation was complete and so she never carried the burdens and responsibilities that fall to fully-fledged members of a community. Much of the time she could follow her natural inclination to remain in solitude praying, writing or sewing, always communing with the Guest of her heart. This fidelity to interior recollection, which was her special vocation, was not effortless. A close reading of what she wrote to others reveals the discipline she imposed on herself.

After little more than three and a half years, Elisabeth's health began to fail and, finally, Addison's Disease was diagnosed. This horrible illness ravaged her body but, for eight months, she endured her passion with extraordinary serenity and fortitude. Only her Prioress was allowed to perceive something of her agony. 'She feels so cowardly, cowardly enough to scream! But the Being who is the Fullness of Love visits her, keeps her company, makes her enter into communion with Him,' Elisabeth wrote to her. Like her fellow Carmelite, Thérèse of Lisieux, Elisabeth knew the temptation to suicide. We must remember that these young women bore their agony without any analgesics or nerve soothing medication. A few days before she died, Elisabeth murmured: 'Everything passes! In the evening of life, love alone remains.'

Judging by what she wrote it would seem (though we cannot be sure) that, although she was not spared days of pain and some even longer periods of interior darkness, luminous faith was, for Elisabeth, the norm. Her Prioress called her a 'soul of one idea.' 'Let God love you,' is what Elisabeth urged on her friends in her correspondence. The vast majority of her letters were written for those living in the world. The words: 'God is love' were for her, as they are in reality, the foundation, the meaning of everything. God is, mysteriously, ineffably a personal communion of love, a Trinity, a threefold mutual self-bestowal, beyond our power to conceive but the fountain of all that is: life and joy leaping up irrepressibly and pouring itself out to share of itself with us. Each of us is a creation of this love; we are here simply so that we can be loved and drawn into this vortex of beatifying love. 'Let God love you' – and in the measure that we do, we are holy with the holiness of Jesus. There is no other holiness, no such thing as 'my' holiness in which I can take satisfaction: 'If you knew how deeply I feel that everything within me is soiled, everything miserable,' she wrote.

God's embrace, God's love makes holy. We can only allow, receive and do everything we can to remove obstacles, to be attentive to God's will – which is always intent on our good, on making us capable of receiving Him:

> We must become aware that God dwells within us and do everything with Him, then we are never common-place even when performing the most ordinary tasks, for we do not live in these things, we go beyond them. A supernatural soul never deals with natural causes but with God alone.

Every human person is a unique creation of love and has his or her irreplaceable function within God's glorious plan of love. There is no such thing as competition; it is senseless to compare this one with that. Each vocation is totally unique, and temperament, circumstances, all the elements that go to make up *my* life are directed towards the shaping of that particular 'form' which is to receive God's love and express His beauty in a way unique to itself, thus becoming a living praise of the glory of His self-bestowing love: 'Each incident, each event, each suffering as well as each joy, is a sacrament that gives God to it.'

Whatever Elisabeth's personal experience of the divine presence, she nevertheless knew the hard struggle of consistently living by faith. As she wrote to her sister Guite, now married with two babies:

> ... cross out the word 'discouragement' from your dictionary of love; the more you feel your weakness and the difficulty of recollecting yourself, and the more hidden the Master seems, the more you must rejoice, for then you are giving to Him ... What does it matter

what we feel; *He* is the Unchanging One ... He loves
you today as he loved you yesterday and will love you
tomorrow.

This fathomless love she contemplated in Jesus, in
love crucified, and longed to be with him in his
total surrender to his Father as she prayed to
receive the life-giving Spirit that would enable her
to pour herself out in selfless love for the world.

> I wish I could tell everyone what sources of strength,
> of peace and happiness they would find if only they
> would consent to live in this intimacy.
>
> (St Elisabeth of the Trinity)

# CHAPTER FOURTEEN

# Carmel, a Dream of the Spirit

Perhaps the greatest contribution St Teresa has made to our Christian heritage is the overwhelming consciousness she had of the apostolate of holiness. Hers seems to have been an age of maudlin introspection: an occupation with one's interior state, of saving one's own soul, avoiding hell, shortening purgatory. Teresa, in her love, broke out of this stifling spiritual egocentricity. She grasped that holiness alone is effective in the world of people. The most brilliant argumentation, preaching or active zeal lead nowhere. They may seem to be effective because they captivate the senses for a time, but only holiness begets holiness. Only those can communicate the kingdom in whom the kingdom already dwells.

Her earliest daughters, those who knew her best, testify that what prompted Teresa in undertaking the reform of Carmel and multiplying her foundations was solely, exclusively, an apostolic drive. This remains one of the essential characteristics of Carmel and its animating force: 'With zeal I have been zealous for the Lord God of Hosts.' (I Kgs

19.10) And, where her daughters were concerned, Teresa grasped that their zeal, the burning jealousy of their love for God, was to be born, nurtured and expanded by constant exposure to the living God: 'My Lord is the living Lord in whose presence I stand.' (I Kgs 17.1)

'Zeal for your house is devouring me,' was said of our Lord in his mortal life. (Jn 2.17) Let us look at that mortal life and at a few sayings which we can be certain he himself uttered in his lifetime. 'How hard it is for those that have riches to enter the kingdom of God,' Jesus says to the rich young man. (Mk 10.23) Note the sympathy of Jesus. He knows how hard it is for a man to surrender to the kingdom. He, in his Father's name, makes this demand on the young man he loves, an unsparing demand. When it is refused he expresses sympathy. By this time he has had ample proof that men and women are not going to surrender, not going to accept his good news, and a growing loneliness envelops him. It is as if he himself stands perplexed: isn't it all too hard for them? 'How narrow is the gate, how strait the way that leads to life, and few there are that find it.' (Mt. 7.14) Did anyone know what he was really talking about? What was he to make of it, this terrible failure to get people to respond? 'I have come to set the world on fire,' he says, frustrated beyond measure because it doesn't happen. (Lk. 12.49) There is only one answer, a dark one: he must cast the burden of it on his Father. One radiant certainty shines out undimmed in the darkness, and this is the Father's will to bring us to himself. This will nothing can thwart except an absolute, determined refusal on our part. Neither our blindness, nor our weakness – the Father can deal with all this, and will deal with it. And then Jesus begins to see that he himself must drown in the depths of human misery, and that through it God will work – how, he does not know. The grain of wheat must die.

When he was planning his campaign, Jesus did an obvious thing, especially when he realized that men and women in general could not respond. He selected a small band of disciples just as, of old, Yahweh had selected a people to keep close to him and to whom he could communicate his secrets so that they might become the means of reaching the whole world. As with this chosen people, so with Jesus' chosen band. They, too, failed and the Servant-Son walked alone, but ah!, not alone, for 'the Father is with me.' And now Jesus' Spirit, no longer circumscribed by human limitation, but filled with all the fullness and power of God, is living in his Church. He can penetrate the most secret recesses of the human heart, yet human hearts remain no less shut now than they were then, no less cowardly or reluctant to receive the kingdom. How, then, does he work? By choosing out those who can receive him and whom he can hope will receive him.

It seems to me that the Carmelite sisterhood, understood in its essence and purity, is a dream of the Spirit. He means it to be a gathering of women prepared to give everything and helped to give everything by the actual organization and way of life. Carmel is meant to be such that everything in it is directed exclusively to God – God alone. God alone written over everything, scored on our hearts: a dream of God, a Mary-life. Here the soil is carefully tilled, waiting day and night to nurture the precious seed. Here is parched earth-inviting fire, craving to be set alight. A dream of God – and it is within my power to realize that dream or to disappoint it. When we think along this line – the line of sheer truth – how dreadful is any impurity in Carmel, any selfishness, slackness, lack of zeal or love.

It is not the great ones of the world God chooses. Look at us ... no one could call us a tribe of spiritual aristocrats! No, we are merely representative of the little folk of the world, and our very natural smallness is important. He wants to show us that the kingdom is for all, that the most precious graces of God are not confined to the highly gifted. Every one of us is an apostle. What we receive, we receive for others. 'Narrow the gate, strait the way'; but if we are courageously fighting our way in at the narrow gate, inevitably we are pulling others after us.

Let each one ask herself: 'Am I living my vocation flat out?' I hope no one answers 'yes!' It would be a sure sign that she was not. As the years go by, though, we can get self-satisfied, not emotionally perhaps and not expressively, but really in that we live as if we were. We are 'good enough', we think. But then we are not fighting our way in at the narrow gate, not striving to enter, not labouring to love. Our hearts should be always asking 'What more, Lord? What do you want of

140

me? What is still wanting? Show me anything that is preventing your love having full scope in me. Show me. Help me to see the showing. Help me to hear the answer to the question: "what still?"'

In what sense is it hard to enter by the narrow gate? Certainly not in any requirement to take on a great burden of rules and regulations, a programme of harsh ascetic practices, a denial of all pleasure and joy in living. Jesus asks nothing like that. There were plenty of people in his time taking on all that for religious motives, yet they were not men of the kingdom. What our Lord asks, what he realized was so bitterly hard for the human heart, was 'conversion': that accepting to turn right round, to be uncoiled from the self-possession, self-centredness and self-orientation that is our native condition, to become God-possessed, God-centred, God-directed. It is what he means by becoming a little one, a child, who alone is capable of receiving the kingdom, of knowing the mysteries of the kingdom. This re-making is God's exclusive work. But we must accept his work, we must allow his divine hand to take hold of us and wrench us into true shape. And we resist with all our might. He knows that only when we are thus re-shaped can we be truly happy. Our misery springs from our self-centredness. Joy and freedom are in God's possession. 'Ah, if only you knew what is for your peace!' (Lk. 19.42)

Let us then open our hearts to God that his Spirit may take possession of us and the dream of God become a reality in our lives – the dream of our vocation – God alone.

CHAPTER FIFTEEN

# Sustained Passion

*It is not the strength but the duration of great desires*
*that makes us great.*

Few saints are better known than Saint Teresa.
Her books, her letters, revealing as they are, are
widely read. But perhaps there is a kind of
knowledge proper to those who actually live the
lifestyle that her genius planned. This is not to
claim that it is a higher, deeper knowledge, but
simply that it is different, perhaps, from what can
be gained from her writings alone. Not only her
books, but also the actual thing that developed as
she set her hand to give new form, new direction
to the Rule of Saint Albert followed by the
Carmelite Order, reveals to us what manner of
woman she was. The Carmel of her devising, the
child of her spirit, is a kind of replica or mirror, not
only of her spiritual but of her human characteristics too. She put her whole self into it; it was
born of the profound spiritual insight that, in turn,
was wedded to her natural gifts and temperament.

Just as an historian can reconstruct an earlier civilization from its present day descendants so, in the measure that Carmel is authentically lived, we could recapture Teresa even without her writings.

A truly amazing feature of Teresa's work of reform was its sureness. Right from the start she knew what she wanted. There was no groping towards some dim vision. No, it was there, clear and shining. Of course, details had to be worked out, tried, modified, changed, but the main structure, together with its inner motivation and direction, were there from the beginning. Teresa attributed this certitude to God himself. In her *Life* she described how it came about that she undertook her great work. For although she had been dissatisfied for some time with the way of life in the Incarnation, the monastery she had entered in her hometown of Avila, it seems not to have entered her head to effect anything so radical as, in fact, she did.

> One day it happened that a person to whom I was talking, with some other Sisters, asked me why we should not become Discalced Nuns, for it would be quite possible to find a way of establishing a convent.

That was the voice of extreme youth; the middle-aged Teresa was more reserved:

> I had had desires of this kind myself and so I began to discuss the matter with a companion ... But for my own part I was most happy in the house where I was, for I was fond of both the house and of my cell, and this held me back.

Then comes what she was convinced was the divine intervention. It was after Communion:

> The Lord gave me the most explicit commands to work for this aim with all my might and main and made me wonderful promises ... that the convent would be a star giving out the most brilliant light.

Thus an idea that she had toyed with, but with no determination or certainty, became an irresistible obsession. The certitude that God willed her to found a convent of perfect observance became the source of her indefatigable determination and drive. That certitude never died. She understood that God has a dream and that Carmel in its perfection is that dream. The Carmel that is to come into being is of immense importance to God; it is to have a vital role in the Church. How could she hesitate? How could she spare herself, or compromise?

'With zeal I have been zealous for the honour of my Spouse ...' If one were looking for a keyword to describe Teresa it would be, I think, this zeal, this 'passion'. It is one thing to speak of 'loving'; it is another to speak of passion. We might say, for instance, that someone 'loves' music, or we might say that music was their 'passion'. Passion implies obsession; all-consuming, devouring one's time, one's energy, one's whole substance. This, surely, is the true implication of this zeal. In applying this to Teresa, we have in mind now the woman she became when she had broken free from her self and her binding attachments and was literally consumed with love, with passion. And it is this passion that is the characteristic of Carmel: not the passion of an hour, of a day, but of a whole lifetime – a sustained passion. Without passion Carmel is not Carmel: it is a dead thing, a mediocre existence deprived of the best human values. Carmel must be all or nothing. It has to be lived to the full or else it is a pitiable existence. Teresa herself recognizes this:

> This house is another heaven if it be possible to have heaven on earth. Anyone whose sole pleasure lies in pleasing God and who cares nothing for her own pleasure will find our life a very good one; if she wants anything more she will lose everything, for there is nothing more to had.

Into the work of reform Teresa poured all her powers, physical, psychic, spiritual, to provide our Lord with utterly true friends who would make His concerns their own and would cease to care at all for themselves. What was true of her was to become true of those chosen for Carmel:

> O my Jesus! If one could but describe how great a gain it is to cast ourselves into the arms of this Lord and make an agreement with his Majesty that I should look to my Beloved and He towards me; that He would take care of my affairs and I of His.

Carmelites were to make it their sole aim to carry out the teaching of Jesus with the greatest perfection, for 'you are my friends if you do what I command you.' They were to study to know his teaching, to know the will of God, the mind of Christ. This is the burden of her teaching: not how to distinguish one mystical state from another, but how to imitate Jesus, how to live with his life. The 'choice' souls who aspire to Carmel must be seeking 'all perfection'. They have received a spark of love that, if fostered, will burst into a flame of passion. Teresa designed the way of life so that everything should converge onto fanning this spark and there is no place in Carmel for what does not press towards passion.

The efficacy, the sanctifying power of Carmel lies in holding in fine balance two seemingly opposed elements: the eremitical and community. There are all the advantages of solitude without its drawbacks; there are all the advantages of community, carefully controlled to ensure its total Christ-likeness. Teresa's understanding of a way that is wholly eremitical in spirit yet lived in community ('yet' is misleading; community is the means of acquiring that truly eremitical heart which is to be alone with God alone) sprang directly form her own experience.

It had been her lot to make her painful ascent to God in an unsupportive community. Far from helping her to give herself to God, it hampered her, indulging her weaknesses. For twenty years she struggled, falling and rising, and eventually won through to a decisive determination to let God have everything. Thus passion was born.

> I desired, therefore, to flee from others and to end by withdrawing myself completely from the world. My spirit was restless, yet the restlessness was not

disturbing but pleasant. I knew quite well that it was
of God and that His Majesty had given my soul this
ardour to enable me to digest other and stronger meat
than I had hitherto been in the habit of eating.

Do Thou strengthen and prepare my soul first of all,
Good of all good, my Jesus, and do Thou ordain the
means whereby I may do something for Thee, for no
one could bear to receive as I have done and pay
nothing in return ... now that I have approached Thee,
now that I have mounted this watch-tower whence
truths can be seen, I shall be able to do all things
provided Thou withdraw not from me.


She had a strong desire for solitude, not so as to
enjoy it (for her 'it is most important for souls
when they begin to practice prayer to start by
detaching themselves from every kind of pleasure,
and to enter upon prayer with one, sole determination, to help Christ bear His Cross'), but as a
way of giving herself more purely to God. She saw
that for her to live her Rule more perfectly is to
help the world that Jesus died for.

Teresa, setting out to found a house – and later
houses – in which the Rule of Saint Albert was to
be kept in its pristine perfection, freely and deliberately chose a very strict enclosure. It was not
just a concession to the times, to the legislation of
the Council of Trent. She chose it as essential for
the particular vocation of prayer to which she
knew herself called by God and which was to be
the vocation of all who would follow her into
Carmel. Teresita, her niece, who had entered
Carmel very young, testified many years later to
what Teresa herself had early outlined to her

brother: 'they will live in the strictest enclosure, never going out, and seeing no one without having veils over their faces ...'

> She (Teresita) said that she knew it was the holy Mother Teresa of Jesus who had started the Order called that of the Discalced Carmelites, and that she had been moved to do so by a desire for the glory of God our Lord and for the good of souls. She wished to try to live, and to get others to live, in the closest possible seclusion and to keep their vows by means of poverty and penance.

It would be easy, on a superficial reading of Teresa's activities, the countless letters she wrote, the vast number of people she knew, to conclude that she had one standard of enclosure for herself and another for her nuns. This was not so. If we look carefully we shall see how set she was on seclusion. The uncomfortable journeys were made even more uncomfortable – tormenting at times – by her insistence that the carts should be covered so that she and her little band of nuns might spend the time as if they were in enclosure. At stopping-places on the way, in lodgings to which they had recourse when they could not immediately take over the house of their choice, she went to elaborate pains to establish some sort of enclosure, appointing one sister to answer the door. Inevitably the business of her foundations took her out; inevitably it was more often she who did so than any of the other nuns; but she was realistic; she knew that the others could lose by it in a way that she would not, for they were mostly young in age and certainly young in the ways of pure love and detachment.

Teresa could have pushed this emphasis on seclusion at an individual level also. She could have founded monasteries based on a complex of cells whose inmates would meet only rarely – after all, this would have been more in line with the primitive Rule she was restoring. Yet with amazing freedom she acted differently, insisting on a strong community life. Hours of solitude, yes; but the Liturgy, meals and daily recreation were to be together. It is this last that must give us pause. She arranged that her hermits should come together twice a day to talk to one another! To understand this let us look again at Teresa's own life. She had experienced the spiritual harm that comes from a lax enclosure and a worldly community, true; but she had also experienced the indispensable benefits of living with others in community. The difficulties she had had to contend with, the struggle to be kind, uncritical, serviceable, truly obedient and humble in community, were what had forged her sanctity. The negative factors were only one side of the picture: she had also been immensely helped by others. Friendship had played a vital role in her spiritual development: to throw this overboard would have been tempting God. He had enlightened her and helped her in countless ways through other people, and she had grasped vividly that this is God's normal means of doing so. How well she writes of this, drawing from her own experience:

It is here, my daughters, that love is to be found: not hidden away in corners but in the midst of occasions of sin. And believe me, although we may often fail and commit small lapses, our gain will be incomparably greater … The reason I say we gain more … is that it makes us realize what we are and of how much our nature is capable. For if people are always recollected, however holy they may think themselves to be, they do not know if they are patient and humble, and have no means of knowing it.

What Teresa is doing is controlling the environment for her nuns. Their vocation is to live in the greatest possible concentration, to spend their whole lives for the salvation of the world. To do this effectively their psychic and spiritual energies must be conserved. Enclosure ensures this can be done. They are preserved from the incessant bombardment of persons and things, each calling for a response. For those whose vocation is to live 'in the world' this is the way they encounter God – a demanding vocation calling for supreme vigilance, generosity and prayer. The Carmelite's way is different. The emphasis in her life is to receive God so that she may give Him, as an empty riverbed receiving those waters with which the world can be irrigated. But she cannot be this empty riverbed, cannot be 'there' for God, unless she is 'clean of heart'. Solitude in itself is nothing. We are no closer to God in physical solitude than in physical proximity to others. To be alone with God alone means an utterly pure, surrendered heart. And the only way to this is through the purification of learning to live with others and loving them. So, though the environment is carefully protected from randomness, it contains within itself everything necessary for human purification and development. It is a little world of its own and amazingly rich, thanks to the rich personality of Teresa.

The Carmelite very soon finds herself 'up against it'. Because everything is streamlined, cut down to a minimum; because there are no diversions and the focus is intense, 'occasions of sin', as present in the world, should be more quickly recognized and more summarily dealt with. Within the small world of a Carmelite enclosure there circulate all the emotions and desires of the human heart. Like everyone else who would be a true Christian the Carmelite has to fight to the death, struggling with her selfishness at every turn: with her ambition, her desire to be successful, esteemed, important. She has to learn to live in submission, for true obedience is a service of love to the community and a drastic surgery to the self-centred ego. She has long hours of unoccupied prayer where, exposed to God, she entreats for light and strength. She has times for being with others, whether at work or at recreation, when the opportunities arise for the practice of virtue in imitation of 'His Majesty.' There is no other way, declares Teresa, over and over again. She knows from her own experience that there isn't. Perfect love of neighbour, which demands utter humility and self-forgetfulness, is all that matters. Some wound to self-love is inflicted, or we have our shabbiness shown up, and there is no escape, for we must return to the solitude and there learn to accept 'humble self-knowledge.' 'I think it is a greater favour if the Lord sends us a single day of self-knowledge, even at the cost of many afflictions and trials, than many days of prayer.'

This passionate lover would have her daughters give everything of themselves to God, be constantly vigilant so that nothing will escape them, no idle deed or thought indulged. Teresa's passion is never up in the air but is always brought down to earth, to concrete expressions of loving desire, affirming in very fact: 'You are all I desire.'

> Never speak without thinking well of what you are going to say and commending it earnestly to Our Lord lest you say anything displeasing to Him ... Never exaggerate ... Never affirm anything unless you are sure it is true.

Teresa was especially concerned with truthfulness and lamented a lack of straightforwardness ('The Prioress is shrewder than befits her vocation ... she has never been frank with me'), and to Gratian himself, addressing him in the third person, she wrote:

> I was wondering if he is not rather careless sometimes in telling the truth about everything ... I should like him to be extremely careful about it ... I do not believe there can be absolute perfection where there is carelessness about that.

All that Teresa had learned over the long, painful years, she urged on her daughters, little things, perhaps, and yet so very important if we would be wholly God's.

Do not pander to your curiosity by talking or asking questions about things which do not concern you ... Do not eat or drink save at the proper times ... Do not complain about food ... Always do what those in your community bid you, if it is not contrary to obedience, and answer them with humility and gentleness ... Never do anything you could not do in the sight of all ... Take great care over your nightly examen ... In all you do and at all times examine your conscience, and having seen your faults strive with the Divine help to amend them. By following this course you will attain perfection.

A Carmelite must be completely detached from herself so that she is free for love. Unless she works for this with all her might and main, making it the passion of her life, there is no point in the enclosed life – Teresa has said so herself.

To be a true friend of Jesus Christ, to share his intimate secrets, to be transformed in him: this is the aim Teresa set for her Carmels. Enclosed in body, the heart of the Carmelite is to be as vast as the heart of Christ. We can watch Teresa labouring for love like this throughout her life. A thoughtful reading of her letters awes one with the impression of a self-expenditure that was complete. This is perfect imitation of Him who is total expenditure. Those marvellous letters, each one distinct, each framed for the recipient with a delicacy that only a Christ-like love and respect could have engendered. She herself exhorted her daughters:

Try, then, Sisters, to be as pleasant as you can, without offending God, and get on as well as you can with those you have to deal with so that they may like talking to you and want to follow your way of life and conversation and not be frightened and put off by virtue. This is very important for nuns: the holier they are the more sociable they should be with their Sisters.

The first field for the exercise of this selfless love is within the community itself. Thus they would comfort, support and enlighten one another, making it easy for one another to love God. The prioress must give leave 'when one Sister wishes to speak to another about their Spouse in order to quicken their love for Him, or to comfort her if she is in some necessity or temptation.' A Teresian Carmel is a happy, gracious dwelling but – let there be no misunderstanding – at the price of constant effort and sacrifice. If they are like Teresa herself then their love will become so easy, so gracious, as to seem effortless and natural. Yet it cost her, as it must cost us all. As she tells us: it was a constant trial to her 'putting up with people of so many different temperaments.'

This love within the community must flow outside it, covering the whole world with its prayers, but specifically touching with its radiance individuals who have contact in one way or another with the monastery:

> Fall in with the mood of the person to whom you are speaking. Be happy with those who are happy and sad with those who are sad ... Don't worry about his being upset: he is always like that. Keep him as friendly as you can.

A striking feature of Teresa's great charity, displayed artlessly in her letters, is her forgivingness. She would allow no 'bad feeling' to exist even towards a person who had no great call upon her. She would put herself to a lot of trouble to mollify, sweeten and heal, and not just for diplomacy's sake – although this was undeniably there at times – but for sheer, gracious love. Even her own daughters wounded her, but how generously she overlooked the hurt and continued to show the same openheartedness, exposing herself and her weakness to them. When one considers how young they were, both in years and in experience of the religious life, it is all the more impressive.

> Where they go wrong, it seems to me, is that, while I put so much love and care into everything that concerns them, they fail in their duty by paying no heed to me and letting me tire myself out in vain. It was because I felt like that that I got angry and would have nothing more to do in the matter thinking, as I said, that I was doing no good – as indeed is the case. But such is the love that I felt, even if my words could be of no avail, I could not wash my hands at all.

It could well be that the constant nausea, weakness and blinding headaches Teresa endured were a direct effect of this unflagging involvement. 'We could often see, to our great distress' wrote one of the nuns,

> ... what inroads they made upon her strength of body. Although these assaults were interior ones they were of such a kind as to leave many marks upon the body ... She told me about this several times after it was all over, and said that, whenever she saw such a soul improving

and making progress, she knew she would have to pay
for it.

Teresa wanted her Carmelites to sacrifice themselves
continually for the world. Strictest enclosure yet
infinite concern.

> Do not let your soul dwell in seclusion or, instead of
> acquiring holiness, you will develop many imperfec-
> tions which the devil will plant in you in other ways,
> in which case, as I have said, you will not do the good
> you might, either to yourself or to others.

She praises those prioresses who were concerned
for the Order as a whole, whereas she reproaches
one for being wrapped up in her own community:

> You know I dislike the way you think that no one can
> see things as your Reverence can. That, as I say, is
> because you are concerned only with your own
> community and not with things that affect many other
> communities as well ... It is a great mistake to think
> you know everything and then say you are humble!
> You do not look beyond the limits of your own house.

A ladylike, leisurely existence was not Teresa's idea
of Carmel. It was to be a life of hard work, for her
nuns were to profess poverty, and the poor must
work for their living. Teresa would seem to have
been possessed of incredible energy. She was
carrying the burden of the foundations, interesting
herself deeply in the affairs of her family, since she
had no option, and in the affairs of many others
who had recourse to her charity. All this involved
constant letter-writing into the small hours of the

morning. On top of this there were her books. Even so, she did not exempt herself from the remunerative work she so strongly imposed on her communities. She would spin whenever she had a spare moment and would take her distaff to the parlour with her for, after all, the fingers can still be busy even while one is talking about lofty spiritual matters! Even if a particular convent was not in need of the income from its work, the Sisters were still expected to work every bit as hard and to give away to the poorer houses what they did not need themselves. They were to be satisfied with the bare minimum of the truly poor: the simplest of food, clothing, furnishings. In actual fact both she and her nuns often found themselves both cold and hungry. Teresa would darn and patch her clothing to make it last as long as it could. On being sent a new freize-habit she wrote: 'I am most grateful as my other one was too full of holes for the cold weather.' It seems, in fact, that 'our Father' (Gratian) had to take it away from her under obedience.

This outward detachment ought to be the natural expression of a detached heart. Not the slightest thing is to be one's own and 'if a Sister is seen to be attached to anything the Prioress must be very careful to take it from her, whether it be a book, a cell, or anything else.' Teresa's own evangelical spirit is reflected in her Carmel: contentment with little; generous human effort; but then no anxiety, only perfect confidence in God who will supply all that is necessary.

Narrowness, rigidity, pettiness, infantilism: these must have no place in these 'dovecots of Our Lady.'

Teresa wanted them to house 'royal souls'. 'I find a puerility in that house which is intolerable', she once wrote. She wanted her daughters to be mature women, even though she often found that they were not. She was not afraid of her rich womanliness: she realized that it was with this that she loved Our Lord and that He positively wanted it, and she trained her nuns to acquire this same capacity. They must abandon childishness and become 'strong men'. Whilst abhorring pretension she admired intelligence: 'it is a great advantage in every way to be intelligent.' She was proud of her daughters' capabilities and administrative gifts – there was to be no slovenliness in her houses as to arrangements, maintenance, or keeping of accounts! Her prioresses, young though they were, were expected to act with maturity: 'never take a step without asking many people's opinions and thinking things over very carefully.' Nor must her Sisters 'think they can first give an order and then countermand it' as though they were a capricious, worldly mistress dealing with her servants.

Other would-be saints have thought it fit to mar what they felt to be an alluring, and therefore dangerous, beauty. Not Teresa. She took delight in physical beauty and charm of manner, though never, of course, giving them undue importance. As everyone testified, she was a veritable heart-stealer herself, of immense charm – and well she knew it! It did not occur to her to dim its radiance or to act in an uncouth way. On the contrary she used it to the full and took thought and trouble to act with human loveableness to win people to a life of goodness. She told her prioresses that they must strive to make themselves loved, not for their own sake but so as to make the yoke of obedience easier for their Sisters. A fine sense of humour she had, too, which she bequeathed to her religious family ('God deliver us from sour faced saints!'). Did anyone have a gift for entertaining? She was to use it to the full. Funny stories were to be stored up to amuse those who were sick. Teresa was quick to see the comic side of situations and quick with a witty response, and she could subtly correct faults by a gently satirical 'leg-pulling':

> Your Reverence is getting what you wanted. God forgive you! Pray to Him that my coming may be good for you and make you less attached to getting your own way. I do not think this is possible – but God can do anything.

Her humour broke forth on one occasion out of her exasperation with Gratian and she told him to 'stop dithering or you will be the death of me!'

Within the limitations of her own times, Teresa wanted her daughters to be well instructed and in contact with the finest theological minds in Spain. She was not averse to the nuns taking an interest in local and national events, provided these were a help to prayer. When the *Moriscos* of Seville were plotting a revolution she wrote to the Sisters there:

> Find out the rights of this and ask Mother Sub-prioress to write and tell us about it ... They [the Sisters at Segovia] think it is a fine thing to be in the middle of all those flags and excitements. If you can, profit by all

the news you are getting and extract some spiritual profit from it. But it is most important for you to consider very carefully how you are to behave or you will find it distracting. I long for you all to be very holy.

Teresa herself had a child's sense of wonder and a vibrant interest in the human scene. If possible – and she was prepared to pay for the privilege – she liked to provide the community with a big garden and lovely views:

> Do you think it a small advantage to have a house from which you can see the galleys go by? We envy you all here for it is a great help towards praising God. I assure you, if your nuns are deprived of it their praises will suffer.

She would never play 'the saint'; her energies and attention were completely absorbed elsewhere. In fact it is evident that, during her lifetime, her daughters never thought of their 'old mother' as a *saint*! One even gets the impression that, at times, they found her to be a bit in the way and – incredible though it might seem to us – young prioresses, longing to try out their own wings, were often enough willing to set their judgement against hers. She exposed herself so nakedly to them, readily revealing her failings, her loneliness, her weakness, her need of love. This sort of thing could blind the unenlightened to her sanctity: it was all just 'too human'. 'How oppressed I have been lately,' she once confided, 'but the oppression passed when I heard that you were well again.' And again, in a pathetic lament to Gratian over her deep hurt and disappointment concerning a deeply loved nun:

> She should realize I am not such a bad Christian! In such a grave matter people living a long way off should not speak against one who would give up her own peace of mind for the good and tranquillity of a single soul.

Readily she would express her sorrow for hastiness:

> I wish I had not made them [her recipient's trials] worse for you. Your Reverence must pardon me, but when I really love anyone I am so anxious she should not go astray that I am unbearable.

In a different vein, she gaily admitted to having enjoyed a journey – because of the company!

> How well I remember what a good time he [Gratian, of course!] and I had together on the journey from Toledo to Avila – which did not do me any harm, either!

Such disarming exposure was, and is, open to misunderstanding and to abuse; but Teresa was heedless of that. This was her way of expending herself. Visitors to Carmelite monasteries today continue to be startled by the down-to-earthness, naturalness, gaiety and spontaneity that they find there. It is the Carmelites' inheritance from this rich and womanly Mother.

Teresa died and there seemed to pass away 'a glory from the earth.' Yet it need not be so interpreted. Her inspiration, her passion, formed a structure, a way of life which, when surrendered to, will engender this same glorious thing: sustained passion burning at the heart of the world, not an emotion but a constant, ever-renewed determination to let God be God, to have simply everything, to be one with 'His glorious Son', receiving the fullness of the Spirit.

# CHAPTER SIXTEEN

# Alone with Him Alone: St Teresa's creative under-standing of eremiticism

'This will always be the aim of our nuns – to be alone with Him alone.'

(St Teresa of Avila, *Life*, ch. 37)

We could not have a purer exposition of true eremiticism, nor a clearer statement of the basic characteristic of the Teresian Carmel. Teresa was restoring a way of life that had been lost; a way of life that had its source in the solitude, the natural enclosure of the Wadi-al-Siah on Mount Carmel in Palestine. We speak of the 'desert of Carmel'. 'Desert' evokes a merciless exposure to the sun and the elements. The Wadi-al-Siah as such did not answer this description but, insofar as the life lived there was authentically eremitical, it would indeed involve such an exposure to reality, and, that means, to God. Similarly, the 'desert' Teresa created for her nuns in no way resembled the harsh terrain of the proverbial desert but was a solitude in which a woman's life could develop and expand.

Teresa's nuns share their daily lives and resources, depend on one another for everything. Moreover, they celebrate Mass and the round of Liturgical Office, and take their meals together. But Teresa goes beyond the cenobiticism of the Albertan Rule and ordains that all the sisters should meet twice a day for recreation, attaching great importance to this. We might have thought that, in her reforming zeal, she would have taken the opposite course and stressed the eremitical aspects of the Rule. On the face of it, it would seem more in tune with her declared aim. Most certainly she did this in the radical nature of her enclosure. Her Constitutions reveal her concern for this complete withdrawal of the community. By means of high walls, grilles and stringent rules, she made a desert in the city, one possibly more protected than the birthplace of the Order. In regard to the life lived within this deep solitude, her nuance is different. Experience has taught her the inestimable value of personal relationships. Significantly, we find nothing in her writings to suggest that the introduction of daily periods of free intercourse were an innovation, still less a mitigation. On the contrary, she confidently affirms that her nuns were living the Rule in all its perfection. But the fundamental obligation of remaining in solitude remains.

'All of that time not taken up with community life and duties should be spent by each sister in her cell or hermitage designated by the prioress; in sum, in a place where she can be recollected ... By withdrawing into solitude in this way, she fulfils what the Rule commands that each one should be alone. No sister ... may enter the cell of another without the prioress' permission.'

And under the same token: 'Let there never be a common workroom'(an almost universal custom in monastic life). The 'Great Silence' ordained by the Rule, stands intact: '... the bell is rung for silence at eight o'clock, and the silence is kept until after Prime the following day. This silence shall be observed with great care.' Teresa's own strict, but humanly balanced, rule of daytime silence further ensured the solitude of each sister. The hours of silent solitary prayer morning and evening, would be – or were meant to be – exposure to God at its purest. For all that a Carmelite lives in community, she will spend a great deal of time alone or, if not alone, in silence.

Ultimately, however, physical solitude must yield to the demands of community.

'It is here, my daughters, that love is to be found – not hidden away in corners but in the midst of occasions of sin; and believe me, although we may more often fail and commit small lapses, our gain will be incomparably greater. Remember I am assuming all the time that we are acting in this way out of obedience or charity: if one of these motives is not involved, I do not hesitate to say that solitude is best.'

(St Teresa of Avila, *Foundations*, ch.5)

And we may add, according to her mind and to the mind of the Rule, that it is the home of the

Carmelite, who has a serious obligation to choose solitude whenever it does not conflict with service to the community.

The desert is not a romantic image. It is the place where we learn to live in *truth*, our self-delusions shattered and illusory securities knocked away. Teresa designed her Carmel precisely to enable her nuns to live in constant exposure to Truth and Love, to be always *there* simply to receive God. This *being there for God* is their special vocation in the Church. *Being there for God* may sound delightful. Teresa knows differently. She writes

> '... the whole manner of life we are trying to live is making us not only nuns but hermits ...'
> (St Teresa of Avila, *Way*, ch.13)

This is in the context of her ascetic teaching on radical detachment from all created things. To be alone with Him alone is, at bottom, to be detached from self, with mind and heart directed to pleasing God only, and this is impossible without generous effort, searching purification and, let us not overlook it, personal maturity.

It is possible for someone to live in physical solitude, to follow a strict rule of life, pray, experience great devotion or desolation, yet remain basically egotistical, undeveloped and emotionally stunted: alone, not with God but with the self and its projections of God. John of the Cross insists that we simply cannot, of ourselves, divest ourselves of our egotism. God has to act both directly and indirectly. Other people are His chosen instruments and we have an absolute need of them in order to mature emotionally, intellectually and spiritually and to learn how to love – our life's greatest task. Living in a community affords us unparalleled opportunities.

Teresa and John share a deep appreciation of the purifying, sanctifying effects of community life if lived as it should be lived. Both excel in showing us how to exploit its potential to the full whilst avoiding its pitfalls – Teresa, principally in the *Way of Perfection* and John in his *Precautions* and *Counsels to a Religious*. To expose ourselves generously to the demands of community life; to refuse to shirk them in any way is to expose ourselves to God, allowing Him to purify us through others, shatter our illusions with humbling self-knowledge, divest us of everything selfish and enable us to love others with a pure, mature, disinterested love. Surely all this is true for whoever would follow Our Lord closely, whatever their form of life.

All human maturation and growth towards union with God demands a creative tension between solitude and community. Understood in a truly spiritual/Christian sense, we cannot have the one without the other, and each thrives in mutual proportion. Each of us must stand absolutely alone before God, assuming full responsibility for our attitudes and choices. At the same time, none of us can come to self-knowledge and maturity without others. The more truly solitary and personal the individual member, the more authentic the community – a genuine communion of mind and heart:

'One as We (the Son with the Father) are One.' (c.f. n17.21).

Teresa's nuns must bring the same wholehearted generosity and fidelity to both aspects of the Rule. It is not a case of choosing to be with others when they want to be and retiring into silence and solitude according to whim. There is an asceticism involved in silence and solitude, as in community living, and this is especially true for certain temperaments. They submit to the asceticism of the Rule whatever their preference. Many times, harassed by the demands of community, they may long to escape to the cell; and there may be times, too, when hurt, troubled and lonely, they crave for human companionship to reassure and comfort them. Fidelity demands that they suffer their little sufferings in solitude, under the eyes of God alone.

If Teresa and John give us abundant instruction as to how to live this creative tension between the communal and solitary aspects of Carmel, Thérèse of Lisieux offers a lived example of total fidelity and the consequences of such a fidelity in her human maturing, her wisdom and sanctity. Understanding the meaning of solitude and being faithful to it, and at the same time forgetting self in the service of the community, enables divine Love to bring to being our true personhood. When that is so then, most truly, are we alone with God alone.

My soul is occupied.
This refers to the soul's surrender of itself to the Beloved in the union of love, wherein it devotes itself, with all its faculties, understanding, will and memory

to His service. The understanding is occupied in considering what most lends to His service, in order that it might be accomplished; the will in loving all that is pleasing to God and in desiring Him in all things; the memory in recalling what ministers to Him, and what may be more pleasing to Him.

(St John of the Cross, *Spiritual Canticle*, st.18)

# CHAPTER SEVENTEEN

# Carmelite Prayer

St Teresa and St John of the Cross write extensively on prayer, but it is hard to discover in their pages anything approaching a distinctive method. Characteristic of Teresa is her freedom in regard to how individuals should pray. She tells us endearingly about her own stumbling journey, her ardent beginnings, the difficulties she encountered, the mistakes she made, and how she was helped by others. We can recall her admiration for the old nun whose only way of prayer was the recitation of vocal prayers – she could do no other – and who yet, in Teresa's estimation, had attained a high state of contemplation ('and would that my own life resembled hers!'). She offers advice deriving from her own experience on how to cope with a restless mind and wandering thoughts, and with times of dryness and aridity; how to distinguish between genuine mystical experience and simulated, self-induced states; on the need to moderate excessive emotion, and so on. John of the Cross is no more specific when it comes to method. He, too, offers guidance, especially for times of

darkness and uncertainty. He analyses the states of
dryness and distaste, offering criteria for discerning
their causes and what should be the soul's appropriate response. However, the lack of specific
method and the fluidity of their approach have
their own significance for an understanding of the
Carmelite way of prayer.

In the *Way of Perfection*, we are allowed to hear
St Teresa in intimate conversation with a beginner
who has no idea how to 'set about it.' Typically,
and significantly, she directs her to the divine
Companion who is present and lovingly intent
upon her. Let her respond to this Friend; let her
ponder on who he is, what he has done for her,
how he has shown his incredible love, what he
wants of her; let her treat him with humble, tender
intimacy. From the very start, without spending
time on intellectual exercises, this beginner is
directed *to relate to a Person* and to reflect on he
who is present. This musing is itself a prayer. Do
not *leave* him to go and think about him! To do
that would be as foolish as breaking from a lover's
arms to study his photograph and his *curriculum
vitae*! This more objective form of meditation is
indeed essential and must not be omitted, but,
according to Teresa's understanding, the hour set
aside for prayer is not the time for it; that hour is
for loving much, not thinking much. John of the
Cross, too, sees that the heart of prayer *is the
presence of God within the soul, a presence that is
not static but an unceasing, positive loving that
prepares us to receive ever more love, an action
that is purifying, transforming, uniting.*

This truth, which lies at the heart of Christian faith, governs our saints' understanding. We have Teresa's image of the soul as a castle, gleaming with the brilliance of a diamond, composed of many rooms encircling one another. In the inmost chamber there dwells the King, the Beloved. Initially the soul cannot perceive her centre, still less enter it, and prayer is seen as a journey inwards towards the centre. The transforming love of the King radiates from the centre, drawing the soul towards itself. Less well known, perhaps, is John's imagery:

> 'We must remember that the Word, the Son of God, together with the Father and the Holy Ghost, is hidden in essence and presence, in the inmost being of the soul ... O thou soul, then, most beautiful of creatures, who so long to know the place where your Beloved is, that you may seek and be united to Him, know now that you are yourself that very tabernacle where He dwells, the secret chamber of His retreat where He is hidden.'
> (John of the Cross, *Spiritual Canticle*, st. 1.6–7)

This secret Guest, the Beloved, is actively seeking the soul, influencing her, drawing her to union with him.

We must strive to grasp and hold on to the bedrock of faith: that God is absolute, unconditional Love. When we say 'love' we do not just mean an ever-kind benevolence bent on our good, a love that gives bounteous gifts, but Love Absolute, giving Itself, whose sole desire is to bring each one of us into an inconceivable union with

Itself, and who is the purpose for which we exist. If we cling to this incontrovertible truth, through thick and thin, we shall keep the right perspective. It becomes obvious that prayer has far more to do with what God wants to do in us than with our trying to 'reach' or 'realize', still less 'entertain', God in prayer. This truth eliminates anxiety and concern as to the success or non-success of our prayer, for we can be quite certain that, if we want to pray and give the time to prayer, God is always successful and that is what matters. We are not outside, as it were, striving for an entrance but in Jesus, our Way, Truth and Life, we have immediate access to the divine Heart. What we think of as our search for God is, in reality, a response to the divine Lover drawing us to himself. There is *never a moment when divine Love is not at work*. 'The Father has never ceased working,' says Jesus, 'and I too must be at work.' (Jn 5.17) This work is nothing other than a giving of the divine Self in love. The logical consequence for us must surely be that our part *is to let ourselves be loved, let ourselves be given to, let ourselves be worked upon by this great God and made capable of total union with Him.*

'How can I begin to commune with this divine Friend?' you ask. Your question reveals your awareness of, or your intention to believe in, his intimate presence. You assume that there is Someone to pray to. The thing, then, is to do all you possibly can to get to know this Someone. Study the Gospels, making use of good commentaries. This work of the mind is indispensable. Try your utmost to get to know Jesus; only you yourself can do this. Don't be content with the trite interpretations with which we become familiar and take as the truth. Jesus *wants* you to know him in truth and can be relied on to help you if you do what you can, humbly, trustfully. *Eat his words,* take them right down into your heart, live with them.

But let us turn now to the time you set aside from all other occupations in order to devote it totally to loving communion with God or with Jesus (it is all the same). Let me share a favourite method of my own, which has helped many others. It is closely akin to what St Teresa was suggesting to her novice. Take a story from the Gospels, let us say that of Jesus' encounter with the Samaritan woman (Jn 4) – John's Gospel is especially helpful for prayer. There you have a wonderful verbal exchange. Read it, recall it, and then believe that you are that person whom Jesus questions and invites you to respond:

'How can I, a poverty-stricken creature give *You* to drink?' you ask.
'You can,' Jesus answers, 'by asking me to give it to you.'
'Help me to know who you are; help me to know, to want, to pay any price for this Gift!'
'You cannot appreciate my Gift. But ask me for it and you will infallibly receive it.'
'Lord, help me! Offer, give me this living water. Draw me to yourself!'

This faith has to be maintained, no matter what our state of feeling, no matter how things *seem*. If we think about it we will realize that there is an implicit but inescapable question at stake here: 'Do I believe in Jesus Christ and in what Jesus reveals of God, which is nothing other than that God is total, unconditional, Self-communicating love?' So, at prayer we are starkly confronted with a choice: Do I stake everything on Jesus or do I choose to rely on my subjective experience?

If the above is true, then our *activity* during a period of personal prayer will consist in maintaining this choice of faith, employing whatever enables us to do this. The accent is not on *our* prayer, our 'performance', but on being there, exposed to God, lovingly eager to receive God and certain that we do so, regardless of how we feel. God is always at work and God's work is God. (c.f. St John of the Cross, *Maxims* 29) Such must be our certain faith. Given this understanding and the resolution to stand by it, there can be no problems about prayer, nor can there be any illusions. Anxieties, problems, doubts about our prayer can only arise when we are viewing prayer essentially as what *we* do for God; and so, of course, what we do becomes very important to us and we are anxious to get it right. Firmly grasping that this is not the case, but that prayer is always rather what God does for us, in us, through us and that our part is simply to be there, as simply and humbly as a child, for Him to act, we are always at peace, never discouraged. We might think that we fail all the time, that we 'can't pray', or that our hour of prayer seems, perhaps, a wash-out from start to finish. But we can smile at ourselves and tell ourselves it doesn't matter: the hour has been full of God because we have wanted to give God that time and receive from Him there all that He has to give.

# CHAPTER EIGHTEEN

# Carmel: A Stark Encounter with the Human Condition

To many people, including Christians, the enclosed contemplative life seems like an escape from the rigours of the human condition. Having lived as a Carmelite for over fifty years, I affirm that, on the contrary, when lived authentically, Carmel is the starkest encounter with the experience of being human. Firstly, I must dispel any illusion that enclosed nuns – and, of course, I speak only from my knowledge of Carmel – know little or nothing of the material anxieties that beset most people at some time or other. To begin with, a Carmelite community is entirely self-supporting, relying exclusively on its own resources. Indeed, I doubt whether there is a community in this country that has not, at some point in its history, experienced real poverty. Moreover, a Carmelite community does not enjoy charitable status. Gradually, over the years, by means of dowries, legacies and occasional gifts, a modest capital may be acquired. However, remunerative work is a matter of necessity if this is to be supplemented, and is by no means only a prescription of the Rule where we are concerned. We have to find ways of earning money and this is not easy from within an enclosure. Industries are laboriously and often painfully established with all the precariousness and vulnerability of small businesses everywhere today. We have to learn a great deal of self-reliance and know what it is to work hard, for, aside from earning an income, there are the ordinary labours involved in maintaining a large household and family. Nor are these burdens that all the members, by reason of age or infirmity, may be able to share. A Prioress and those other officials who are more directly acquainted with the financial affairs of the house and its running costs may know many a sleepless night. And with reason.

Secondly, the community depends for its existence on a steady intake of new members that may, or may not, be forthcoming. It is autonomous and cannot, as a matter of course, be reinforced from elsewhere. Vocations are God's business. We can only wait on divine providence, never wholly blind to the possibility that the time may come when we are no longer viable as a functioning Carmel and must close.

But if the community as such is no stranger to insecurity, neither is the individual religious. She does not handpick the companions with whom she spends her entire life, and yet vows herself to them for better or worse, bound as stringently as a married person. If things are not to her liking, if trouble strikes, she is not free to change residence, but must remain dependant on this particular group for every material need as well as for love and emotional support. A Carmelite has to learn to trust God blindly through the sacramentality of her community.

These more obvious concerns emphasizing our dependancy, pressing as they are, far from exhaust its extent. Basic to human experience is the awareness of limitation, even of helplessness, and of how little control we have over our life: the events that overtake us, the circumstances that surround us and even over that intimate part of us, our body. And what about our psychic, emotional life? How inexorably even this reflects our inheritance, our conditioning. We have been worked on before ever we were born, with no awareness, no consent of our own. Age brings not lesser, but deeper awareness of dependency and insecurity.

I would like to suggest that one of our most powerful drives, and that which absorbs our attention and energy most of all, is the diminishment of these experiences of helplessness and the gaining of more control over our life. No one can deny that this, in itself, is a healthy thing and essential; but in spite of all our efforts there is little doubt that we shall meet with defeat after defeat. Fear is our most pervasive emotion, deriving from the experience of contingency. One way or another, we are always striving to reassure ourselves, to keep fear concealed or at bay. We have countless ways of doing this: incessant activity, initiating fruitless discussions, creating noise and diversion, seeking the person or persons who will provide an illusion of safety or mitigate our feelings of personal inadequacy, to name but a few. We may lull the inner anxiety but never get rid of it.

Assuming the basic correctness of this diagnosis, we shall discern how important it is for our well-being, maturation and contentment, our ability to love and support others genuinely and to play a positive role in the human community, that we come to terms with this inner anxiety. This means, in effect, coming to terms with our fundamental helplessness, uncovering its meaning and using it creatively.

As Christians, we have the blessed certainty through Jesus Christ of our unshakeable security in the divine love. Each of us is loved by God with a limitless, unconditioned and unconditional love that we can never destroy or even diminish. We are loved into existence; cherished in our existence; affirmed absolutely in death and beyond. This love is independent of our merit or demerits. Nothing whatsoever can separate us from this love. For it is the breadth; it is the length; it is the height and it is the depth – there is nowhere beyond it, above or below it. It is All: the limitless ocean that encompasses our tiny, threatened, fragile yet infinitely precious self. This is not merely impersonal, protective benevolence but a love that gives self, that offers inconceivable intimacy and that seeks reciprocity. We can never define or draw a line around what God will do for each one of us. We are exposed to the infinite. Against this truth what does our sense of impotence matter? In genuine faith – which must, of course, be worked for –

and in that surrender of self which is faith in act, we begin to discern that, far from our helplessness being a human misfortune, something that ought not to be, it signals a limitless calling and is the other side of a vocation that goes beyond what can be perceived by mind and sense. To accept it is to assent to our vocation, to becoming who we truly are, to being truly human. We are made for union with the divine, nothing less. We are called to share the life of God. Our restlessness, our insatiable longings, our discontent and experience of helplessness are to be traced to our divine destiny. Commitment in faith to this truth is to destroy existential anxiety. Faith alone can overcome the world and the threat the world imposes. It does not follow that we lose the feeling of anxiety and fear – we would be the poorer for that – but these now play a role that is creative not destructive. Fear can cripple, paralyse, prompt us to shirk and evade life. Faith enables us to live with reality, braving its challenge.

Living myself within the enclosure of Carmel, accepting its discipline and trying to understand its living spirit (and this, to begin with, under a regime when the customs, assumptions and attitudes of past centuries remained virtually unchallenged, through to an evolution in the spirit of Vatican II), has left me with the conviction that Carmel offers an extraordinarily effective means for experiencing the reality of our humanity. To claim this is, at the same time, to claim that it is a most effective means of surrendering the whole person to God. So convinced am I of this that I am ready to define

Carmel as an intense experience of human existence and its innate poverty, containing within it a summons of faith not to evade but to enter through it into a total trust, a leap of the self into divine love which is the essence of union with God.

I cannot claim that what I have described is universally accepted, that Carmel is or always has been understood in this way. Our hagiography alone would give this the lie. But, for the purposes of this consideration, I would like to take an image from horticulture and offer an interpretation of Carmel in terms of a 'forcing house'. To choice plants the forcing house offers the perfect conditions for sturdy growth. However, it also offers the same conditions to noxious weeds. No doubt blatant vice will not be found within a Carmelite community and, if it should appear, would be eliminated quickly. But, too easily, the roots of vice pass undetected because their manifestations are on so small a scale as to seem insignificant, being 'merely human'. If these are generally accepted as normal, then only a very enlightened, very directed heart will see them for what they are and be able to uncover them. Both St Teresa of Avila and St John of the Cross, with their keen vision of God and of the human heart, have much to say about these seemingly small faults which have their roots in our pervasive selfishness. They understood Carmel to be precisely a way of life in which this selfishness can be purged. Similarly, the abundant literature concerning St Thérèse of Lisieux, which affords a lively picture of the reality of life within her Carmel, shows how it proved to be for her

186

just such a forcing house in which, through her intuitive understanding of the charism of Carmel and surrender to it, she made rapid progress in sanctity. At the same time, an honest appraisal of this evidence in Thérèse's case also reveals how the same conditions fostered weeds in others. Thérèse, young though she was, was one who swam courageously against the tide. She knew the Rule and kept it, regardless of others' carelessness; recognized evil when she saw it and was prepared to wield her sword even when the powerful figure of the Prioress was involved or, perhaps more painfully, her own beloved blood sisters.

The dangers of narrowness and myopia that can be fostered among a small group of women who are dependant on one another for stimulation and challenge are not the only ones to be encountered in a 'forcing house'. Concentration on spiritual things, a hallowed tradition, the inherited vocabulary and manners of the community, the religious habit and name, can all encourage a 'saintly' posing. The 'saintliness' in question can be impressive, and it would be temerity to deny it all reality. The subject may be by general standards genuinely virtuous and generously self-denying. At the same time, one detects a certain self-consciousness, a somewhat complacent awareness of being spiritually interesting and beautiful, in spite of constant protestations to the contrary, and a concern for a spiritual image rather than for gift of self to God and the self-forgetfulness that this engenders. Such spirituality seems to deny the raw stuff of our humanity and what are generally termed negative emotions – such as anger, jealousy, hatred, resentment. As these emotions feel besmirching and sinful to her, they are automatically repressed. In particular, sexuality is denied its full, wide-ranging reality. A mistaken notion of the Carmelite ideal to live for God alone – 'alone with God alone' – leads to a harmful rejection of created and human values. The pitfalls of Carmelite enclosure are the inevitable risks involved in a life-style that offers immense creative possibilities, provided only that it is understood and organized wisely.

Strict enclosure is, of course, Carmel's dominant feature. Carmelites leave the enclosure only when really necessary and, in practice, this largely means for medical attention. Their entire life is passed within a defined area, and in consequence they are deprived of manifold means for the development of the human person. It is God's will that we become sexually integrated, mature persons and we may not, in God's name, neglect this basic obedience. Therefore we must ensure that our enclosure holds within it the possibilities for human development. The principal means towards this are, I suggest, first of all real, warm relationships, genuine intimacy and friendship. But in addition there must be such elements as a wide range of reading matter to further intellectual and emotional development, an informed awareness of the processes of psychological growth, and the exercise of personal responsibility. Enclosure is not meant to cripple us but to foster a high quality of life that will allow for deep reflection and for the 'experiencing of experience'. Constant exposure to sensory, emotional and intellectual impressions can lead to a diminishment of actual experience. Undigested experience, however, when events, encounters, feelings and reactions float through us leaving no trace, is not experience. Enclosure, with its built-in forms of censorship, enables us to sift, garner, absorb, thus conserving energy for what matters. Awareness and sensitivity are likely to increase, perhaps to painful proportions, and we will be far from immune to the sufferings and cares of others.

Within the desert of enclosure, a Carmelite lives her life with a community, and here is another powerful agent of self-revelation as a human being and stimulant to growth. A Carmelite community is carefully organized: periods of solitude are built into its daily life and silence is the order of the day, though, of course, the silence is not absolute. There are those exchanges essential to work and the smooth running of things, for instance, to attending to needs, and to offering and receiving spiritual and emotional support. Each evening we all gather, without fail, for an hour's chat, attaching great importance to this friendly exchange. There is also constant, wordless communication when we are at liturgical prayer, or when dining together or meeting in passageways and, ideally, this silent communication emits warmth, gentle courtesy, respect and concern. However, no matter how high the level of genuine charity, the reality of our individuality makes some friction and misunder-standing inevitable. Since the Rule does not allow for 'on the spot' explanations or sorting out of differences this calls for trust in one another. Our

189

only recourse is to take our little smarts, our fears, our loneliness and feelings of being undervalued and perhaps unloved into solitude and face them with Our Lord. It is such a human tendency when our self-esteem is wounded and our confidence undermined to run to someone who will give us the comforting assurance that we are the nice person we thought we were!

This fine balance of solitude and community living allows a keen self knowledge to emerge and we are challenged to confront dark, painful areas within ourselves. There is nowhere to run if we would escape. We experience keenly that we are weak and sinful. Of course, self-love can always find bolt-holes, even in Carmel, but the opportunities are reduced. We can find peace and contentment only in accepting our human indigence, in loving trust in God. If I may put it so, 'success' in Carmel lies precisely in facing up to the unlovely reality of our human nature – unlovely only to ourselves and our proud expectations – and in our peaceful acceptance of it.

When we enter Carmel, we have deliberately chosen a situation where helplessness is accentuated. It is a common experience for a postulant to seem to regress. Hitherto she has probably shown competence in her profession, achieved a certain status and sense of poise, and enjoyed the independence of her own house or flat. One step through the enclosure door and all these are left behind and, with them, the *persona* that she has not yet recognized to be a *persona*. Of course, each person is different, and not all experience the shock with such intensity; but the fact remains that everyone, sooner or later, has to be stripped down to who she really is. Needless to say, no one takes it upon herself to do this for the entrant. On the contrary, the superiors and the community in general are invariably full of solicitude and under-standing of her 'overthrow' and the pain involved. It is the reality of the life-style itself that effects it – and it is meant to do so. It can happen that a woman, seemingly mature and able to support and counsel others, now finds herself reduced to tears over 'nothings', craving appreciation and affection. Not surprisingly, there can be a temptation to run away, convinced that it is a crazy way of life and certainly not the way of life for her! 'I was not like this outside,' is the common moan. Her superiors will gently insist that she was, but that the immaturity and weakness were covered over: she had found countless ways of hiding them from herself and from others. In Carmel she must face them and this is a blessed grace. Much depends on the community's attitude. If the community is composed of people who live within their own truth and who recognize the action of God in such experiences, the postulant or novice will be given every chance to grow gradually into her own reality; there will be no harmful repression and, through prayer, fidelity to the Rule and the loving support of others, she will learn to live from her own centre and not be governed by her innate fears, inner compulsions and the expectations of others. Carmel undoubtedly offers a hard but healthy regime, and time and time again we see those who have embraced it finding contentment and a sense of meaning such as they never knew before. In a short time they discover themselves strangely changed in outlook: no longer longing for the good things they formerly appreciated and enjoyed, but aware that they hold within themselves a gift that surpasses them all. This can continue even in the midst of turmoil and affliction. Growth in self-knowledge is not over and done with in the first few months, of course, but goes on through life. Yet, to my mind, we cannot sufficiently stress the importance of understanding this painful phenomenon, of welcoming it and exploiting it to the full as that which, if truly accepted, opens us fully to divine love. In theory this is understood, but the actual reality is so ugly that the temptation to baulk it in some way is inevitably strong – though often subtle.

We have not finished here with the impoverishment and sense of helplessness to which Carmel is meant to bring us. There is a deeper dimension still and this encircles prayer itself. Carmel, we say, is a life of prayer: prayer is our primal duty to which all else is subordinated and directed. Most of us cherish the illusion that to give oneself up to a life of prayer will, sooner or later, bring returns. We shall, we imagine, become more spiritual, feel better about ourselves and human life in general; we shall be, at least to some degree, lifted out of the common rut. As I have already suggested, this illusion can be fostered by a whole community and to some extent can seem reality. In her perceptive study of St Thérèse, *The Hidden Face*, Ida Görres demonstrates how Thérèse resisted to her dying day, with all her passion for truth, the temptation to 'saintliness' pressed on her by her *milieu*: to be careful of her image, to say saintly, edifying things, to pretend. If proof were needed of this pressure we would only have to consider the censoring of her writings and of all witnessing to her life, carried out after her death by those who thought they understood her best. Everything that was 'too human', that did not quite fit the common image of holiness, was carefully suppressed. We came to understand Thérèse fully, in all her splendid humanity and glorious truth, only when the well-meaning, venerable guardians of her image were dead. A genuine life of faith of necessity destroys illusion. It needs none. It seeks the truth with passion.

Carmelites have no external apostolate. It is our faith-informed conviction that a life given wholly to God is the most effective apostolate. One for whom God matters supremely and who is deeply concerned for others, keenly aware that love for God is inseparable from love of the neighbour, will not find acceptance of this apparent non-contribution easy. It will demand a constant reaffirmation of faith in her own vocation if she is to resist the temptation to compensate in some way. It might not be so difficult to accept if one had a sense of doing one's own job well, of being a successful pray-er! This is unlikely. What happens if we feel we do not pray, that our prayer is hardly prayer, so poverty-stricken it is, so lacking in all comforting feedback, all high sentiment? How often one hears the anxiety voiced: 'I feel I do nothing for God. As a person vowed to a life of prayer I am a failure,' and so forth. Now this, I believe, is where we touch the very heart of our vocation in the Church, the point where it bears witness to the truth that all must come from God, that all is pure gift and that as human beings we are there only to receive Love, to be 'done unto' in gracious mercy and love. It is in this way that we glorify the pure, totally gratuitous love of God. Unless every Christian's heart lies thus at the feet of divine Love, humbly waiting, trusting, claiming nothing, relying only on what Love will do – the Love which has shown itself as such in Jesus – he or she may be religious, but not truly Christian. A Carmelite is called to live out this human vocation – synonymous with the Christian vocation – in an absolute way, becoming a glad receptivity for all that comes to her in a radical renunciation of every spiritual claim, every reassurance coming from the self. Thus it reminds us all of what is the heart of the matter. It is no easy vocation. I recall how, as a young Religious, suffering acutely from the feeling that as a Carmelite I was an utter failure, having nothing whatever to offer to God, I gradually perceived this to be precisely what the vocation is about, its very heart. I was to receive and to believe I had received without any token thereof. I was to accept to have nothing to give, to live always with empty hands. My giving could only be in allowing God to give. I recall with emotion and deep gratitude how I found this insight wonderfully confirmed by Thérèse in her letters, an English translation of which had just been published. Since then it has grown until it has taken over completely, and I realize how careful we must be, if we would be true to our vocation, not to evade, not to seek in anyway to overcome this profound awareness of spiritual inadequacy or pretend it is not there. The form of 'saintliness' that held glamour for the contemporaries of St Thérèse is hardly likely to be ours; but we shall not lack the urge to find ways and means of somehow making the life-style more interesting and ourselves more satisfactory, of 'doing it better'. Perhaps our lure today lies in constant discussions about it, in unrealistic ideas of on-going formation, in more obvious involvement in Church affairs, in stimulating mental and emotional awareness of the world's sorrows. Obviously these must have their place; but everything depends on the motivation, in what we are hoping to achieve by them. Nothing must be allowed to take from us or even to mitigate our poverty, our helplessness, our 'nothingness'.

This is not a lovely spiritual ideal, but an experienced reality that can be loved and must be loved only because it opens ourselves and the world to the purifying, transforming, beatifying love of God.

CHAPTER NINETEEN

# Consecrated Life

It is the privilege of all of us in religious life to have been called out of the Christian community to serve that community in a special way, not primarily by the ministry we fulfil but by our public profession of belonging absolutely to God; by our lived affirmation that the love of God, the fulfilling of God's will, are our supreme and only concern, and that God is worth the offering of our whole life. That, surely, is what we mean by consecrated life: the daily intention and effort to live for God alone and not at all for ourselves.

To have been moved to do this – to want to do this no matter how feeble the wanting – indicates divine, not merely human, inspiration. Human nature of itself does not produce such desire. What I have to say deals only with this ground level of our consecrated life and, I believe, applies to everyone of us, be they young, old or middle aged; a member of a modern, vibrant community or of an older institution that seems called upon to die; whatever the ministry they fulfil.

There must be many ways of speaking about this ground level, but I draw on my own tradition and experience. It is the truly contemplative, mystical way. I hold the unswerving conviction that the mystical way, properly understood, is identical with genuine Christian discipleship and with what we mean by true faith and a life of faith. 'God has no need of our works but only of our love.' This is a well-known dictum of Thérèse of Lisieux and, when properly understood, it takes us down to this bedrock level of Christian existence.

With a view to this, I have decided on three headings: the overarching one of FAITH and, under that, two of the principle ways in which faith is lived – PASSIVITY and EXPOSURE. I believe that these concepts cover all.

It is my experience that faith does not get the attention it ought to have. Too often we take it for granted that we have faith and that we live by faith. No doubt this is true in an overall sort of way. But faith, to be real faith, is incessant, always operating, governing the entirety of life with nothing whatever left out: governing our thinking, our point of view, the forming of judgements, our actions. This is impossible without enormous, specific attention. Our natural, spontaneous way of acting (and with religious people it can pass unnoticed when it seems harmless and neutral) is to live by what our feelings tell us is the truth of things. By our feelings, I mean our general consciousness: how we experience and perceive ourselves, others, events and, of course, God. We tend to judge ourselves (do we not?) – our prayer, our spiritual life, our progress – on how it seems to us, and we just assume this is the reality. In Carmel we teach the importance of taking a stand against this natural propensity of trusting our own consciousness to tell us the truth about reality. And how hard a lesson it is for many! It has to be repeated over and over again and, indeed, I have to keep reminding myself! Christianity stands on objective truth, not on subjective perception, intuition, reasoning or whatever, whether collective or individual. It is my experience that this absolutely basic fact is, in practice, often woefully overlooked. We Christians must look to Jesus, and to Jesus alone, for our vision of God, ourselves, others and the world around us.

Jesus is the prime object of our faith: Jesus, the full human expression of God's God-ness, of what makes God to be God. And how different this is from the notions of God that the human mind and heart produce of themselves. We come to know in Jesus that the REALITY, the MYSTERY in which we are immersed, the nature of which we could know nothing unless disclosed to us, loves us. We are not loved as a collective mass, but as individuals. This is the object of our faith. This is what it means to believe in Jesus Christ. If we truly believe it, then we hold on to the fact that we are utterly safe and secure in this love – the one absolute of life. We cannot lose it, cannot escape its enfolding: it is there for us, one with our existence. This love, we see in Jesus, is not mere benevolence, the will to do us good, to shower good things on us. This is that absolute love that must be the gift of self. God gives God's very Self to each one of us as our perfect fulfilment, our only fulfilment. We cannot imagine such love, for it exceeds everything the human mind and heart can grasp; but we can get faint intimations of it in our experience of human love. It is not meaningless to us. Jesus gave the name of Father to this Love and he strains to get us to trust this Father utterly. This is what it means to be his disciples in truth. Faith means living all the time by this truth, it means a constant surrender to it, a desire to receive it. And this is the mystical life: the human person becoming more and more receptive to the inflowing of divine love which, as it enters, of necessity purifies and transforms.

Is such faith easy? Of course not, and Jesus knew it was not. The Letter of the Hebrews calls Jesus our pioneer in faith and shows Jesus himself struggling with the opacity of experienced Reality and the hiddenness of God. 'When the Son of Man comes, will he, do you think, find faith left on earth?' (Lk. 18.8) Such was his poignant reflection towards the end of his life. To believe steadfastly in Jesus, to take him as our only Way, our only Truth, our only Life, seems, as often as not, to be going clean against our whole experience of reality. But such is real faith, based on objective truth, not on what derives from the human mind and heart.

*Passivity*

What I mean by passivity is the attitude of heart and mind (an attitude that cannot just come of itself but must be conscientiously cultivated) that remains always on the receiving end in the divine relationship. It means a practical, not merely notional, grasp that our God is incessantly on offer, always there, waiting to be taken in and received. It means a rejection of every impulse of anxiety about our relationship with divine love as though it has to be established, merited, summoned to us. When we, earnest people for whom God really matters, look into our hearts, do we not find that our basic question is: 'What can I do for God? What can I give to God?' There is only one answer – God's answer: 'Nothing, beloved! Only receive with glad heart what I give, and that is myself. The greatest gift you can give me is the trust that lives by this truth.' It is, of course, what Jesus is saying when he tells us we must have the heart of a child in regard to God. I wonder whether we take seriously enough, we grown men and women, the stress that Jesus puts on being a child in order to receive what God has to give? It means God can come fully only to the little one. It means renouncing all ideas of our own spiritual impor-tance, of what we do for God, what we give to God, our own supposed goodness and virtue. It means casting aside any concern for that image of ourselves, so precious to ourselves, that we are indeed truly spiritual men and women. Julian of Norwich maintains that, in this life, we can have no other stature than that of childhood. I think that when Jesus takes the child in his arms, sets him in front of himself, pointing to him as a model, it is to himself he is pointing. His inmost heart was always that of a child and that is why he could live with such freedom, courage and self-squandering. To my mind this is the nub of the truly Christian faith, this grasp that all is gift and our work is simply to receive, to learn how to receive. Certainly, when I myself get the spiritual 'fidgets' and become anxious about myself and my life, I find my answer in simply saying to myself: 'You are only a child!'

We must understand, practically, that we are being moulded, shaped by divine love as clay in the hands of the potter. We must give up trying to make ourselves into a nice shape for God. The truth that all is given, all is done for us, lies behind the sacraments, Catholicism's most precious insight. We do not make our worship; we do not make reparation; we do not atone; we do not establish a relationship with God, erecting our own ladder between heaven and earth. All this is done for us and we go to receive it, enter into it and lose ourselves in it. At the root, then, there must be this attitude of passivity and, from this passivity, a life of outpoured love for others. Think again of a vessel – a bowl. Perhaps we see ourselves as pouring into it our apostolic work, our prayer, our liturgical worship, and holding it up as our offering to God? No. The bowl's meaning consists in remaining at the divine fountain – always, always! – and in receiving what God gives. And we can be sure that it is constantly filled, whether we know it or not, and that its contents overflow whether we know it or not. 'Of his fullness we have all received.' (Jn: 1. v.16) We have, and can have, no fullness of our own. Our vocation is to remain an empty bowl at the fountain and this means we

202

sacrifice the desire to feel full, of trying to find ways of giving ourselves a sense of fullness, of spiritual richness. Such a sense of fullness is more likely to tell us that we are full of ourselves!

## Exposure

The faith that believes in the continuing self-offering of God to each one of us necessarily trusts reality. How else can divine love come to us save through life as it unfolds? This is what I mean by exposure: a practical trust that God gives God's own self here and now, in these circumstances, in this situation. Such a faith refuses evasions or shirking; it refuses the often subtle ways of manip-ulating life. As consecrated persons, and most specifically as Religious, we have given up the control of our own lives. We have been placed, disposed of. We do not place ourselves; we are no longer our own mistresses. We have been handed over and belong to others and this means, primarily, to our community and, more extensively, to the community of the Church.

The self-surrender inherent in religious vows and consecration can become a reality insofar as we never give up trying to be faithful, aiming always at total gift. Nevertheless, it can become a myth. It seems to me that of all persons, those consecrated to God such as we are, who have handed over the control of our lives and, in loving trust to Love's sworn fidelity, have put ourselves in a state of great dependency, can be absolutely certain that God ensures each one of us of this: that in my situation, here and now, I have simply everything that can open me to divine Love, nothing is wanting to me. It may not seem like that. We may be tempted to think: 'If only…'. Let it be seen as a temptation. Let us learn to use everything, waste nothing. A true disciple is always awake, always watching to welcome the Beloved. Divine love offers itself in the 'sacrament of the present moment,' to quote de Caussade's immortal phrase. The accent is not on what I can give to God, how I can serve God, but 'what do YOU want me to do?' and the answer is in front of our noses, in what needs doing here and now, rising out of the actual situation we are in. Looking at this aspect of trusting reality as the vehicle of God, and exposing ourselves to it with undefended heart, perhaps nowhere are we more tested than in regard to our experience of ourselves, our emotional and spiritual flaws, our sense of inadequacy, our sense of being a spiritual failure – or whatever the ailment. Let's just lump it all under the heading of: accepting to be human and not divine, or even angelic. When we are longing for God, truly in earnest, eager to work for others, our lives, our selves seem so insignificant, pathetic, paltry. Something must be wrong somewhere and we set about trying to feel better. Perhaps we look for the spiritual guru who has the magic answer to prayer, or try to get ourselves into what we think would be a better situation for loving God, or think up unrealistic plans for our apostolate. No doubt there are instances when the Holy Spirit is behind such movements, but I think that we must be very, very wary. Often enough what we are looking for is not how to love God better, but how to feel better about ourselves, purer, more fervent, more spiritual. We in Carmel, as you can imagine, know all about the experience of feeling unspiritual, paltry, doing nothing for God. Maybe we all secretly nourish or have nourished the expectation that closeness to God will make us feel marvellous, will lift us up out of the dragging poverty of ordinary human experience. God will purify this selfish motive if we allow Him to, and if we refuse to evade our own reality and the reality in which we find ourselves.

Let me stress a little more the supreme importance of refusing to evade our own personal poverty, refusing to be discouraged by it. Only too easily, self-disgust and discouragement become spiritual waste. I think it is of utmost importance to use everything for loving. After all, our lives are made up of 'nothings!' We can be on the lookout for the big occasions and let slip the hundreds of little opportunities when divine love is asking to be let in. Nothing about us is hidden from the loving, compassionate eyes of God, but when we are feeling miserable within, shamed, silly, dirty even, we hide away. God isn't in all this, we implicitly assume. But God *is* in all this, to us, contemptible stuff. We lose very much by this lack of childlike trust. Through what is happening to us, we are brought to face with our sinfulness, our selfishness, our inadequacy or whatever it is. Yet this is God's moment. It is, I believe, in the constant, almost hourly choices that these humiliating, self-revealing experiences afford us, that true holiness and union with God is brought about. I'm sure that what God longs for us to do is never to stop looking into His compassionate eyes. Nothing is too small, pathetic or shameful to be used for love.

Faith lives nakedly exposed to God in the experience of reality, in the experience of ourselves, in the experience of prayer. I have always found inspiration and support in the Jesus of Hebrews: He who is extolled as God's own Son; appointed heir of all things; through whom the world is created; who reflects the glory of God and bears the very stamp of God's nature, upholding the universe by his word of power and to whom God says, 'Thy throne, O God, is for ever and ever.' This is the One who crosses the frontier into the finite and takes, not angelic nature but human nature in all its weakness. He becomes most truly one of us: like us in all things, beset by weakness, tempted in every way as we are. He is not concerned with being angelic, but with being human. If this is the choice of the Son of God, how can we despise our frailty; how can we aspire to be angelic or divine according to our own notions of the divine? Jesus teaches us to love our poverty. Jesus teaches us how to live divinely from within our human weakness, not above it or apart from it, and in the midst of temptation. Son of God though he was, he learned obedience through what he suffered.

To my mind, Jesus' primal obedience, as is ours, was to accept to be a human being, together with all that this entails. He had to learn by sheer experience how hard a vocation it is. We are told that he learned it, not by what he did, but by what he underwent, and this is significant. It is the only way. Only God knows what a human being is; only God can create a human being and this God is intent on doing. We, like Jesus, have to shut our eyes, give up the controls, allow God to work and say, with Jesus, our 'yes, yes!' It is thus that we cease to be in control by trying to be our own god, our own creator, and we accept, as He did, to be human: wholly contingent; with no answer, no fulfilment in ourselves; an emptiness that looks to infinite love for its completion. Because of Jesus we, too, can learn obedience, learn to accept with all our hearts the painful but wonderful vocation to be a human person. This 'yes' of Jesus is that all-powerful word that upholds the universe, taking it to God. And our struggle to say, to be, a constant 'yes' is, I believe, our greatest work for the world.

Finally, we are talking about trying. We can do only that, try: try to believe; try to trust; try to say 'yes'. We do not look for success so as to be assured that we do believe, do trust. We give ourselves over completely to divine love. We live for God, not for ourselves.

# Acknowledgements

'Some Reflections on Prayer' was first published in *Mount Carmel* (Advent 1994).

'Growth in Prayer' was first published in *The Way* (October 1983).

'Faith, Trust, Surrender to God' was first published in *Compass* (May 1990).

'If you knew the gift of God …' and 'Prayer in the Trinity' were first published in *Priests and People*.

'Distractions in Prayer' was first published in *Bible Alive*.

'The Way to Perfection' was first published in *The Tablet* (16 October 1982).

'Doctor of the Dark Night' was first published in *The Tablet* (14 December 1991).

'St Thérèse of Lisieux and the Holy Child' was first published in *Priests and People* (December 2001).

'St Elisabeth of the Trinity' was first published in *Bible Alive*.

'Carmel, a Dream of the Spirit' was first published in *Mount Carmel* (Spring 1986).

'Sustained Passion' was first published in *Mount Carmel*.

'Alone with Him Alone' was first published in *Mount Carmel* (July–September 1999).